HOW TO STOP NEGATIVE THOUGHTS:

What My Near Death Experience Taught Me About Mind Loops, Neuroscience, and Happiness

BARBARA IRELAND

Book Design by Boots

First Printing, 2016
ISBN: 1535089547
ISBN-13: 978-1535089548

The Mind Loop Group
4111 East Madison Street
PO Box 141
Seattle, WA 98112

http://www.HowToStopNegativeThoughts.com

DISCLAIMER:

The author is not a licensed psychologist. The ideas, techniques, and suggestions in this book are not intended as a substitute for consulting with your physician. The author is not liable or responsible for any loss or damage allegedly arising from any information or suggestion in this book.

The cases and quotations used in this book are based on interviews with real people; however, the details have been changed and cases have been merged together to protect their privacy.

HOW TO STOP
NEGATIVE THOUGHTS

To all the brilliant authors, neuroscientists, biologists, psychologists and thought leaders who have inspired me, and made my life better because of their work.

And to anyone still suffering from "Mind Loops":
May this book help you find overflowing peace and happiness in your life.

And to H.P. with love.

CONTENTS

INTRODUCTION:.. 1

Why You Need To Read This Book.........................1

FAQ: For the Curious and the Doubtful............................ 3

My Mind Loops Story 8

The Many Sides of Mind Loops 10

The Turning Point 13

PART ONE: WHAT ARE MIND LOOPS? **17**

Mind Loops 18

Mind Loops Are Sticky and Contagious 20

How Much Are Mind Loops Running *Your* Life?

   – Take the Quiz 22

You're In Good Company 25

You CAN...28

Can't Wait To De-Loop?.................................... 29

Open the Parachute 30

You. Are. Great... Period. 31

PART TWO: MY NEAR-DEATH JOURNEY 33

A "Premonition"...36

Intensity..37

The Terror Begins 41

The Teaching Begins..42

The Question That Altered My Life Forever....................45

PART THREE: HOW TO GET OFF THE NEGATIVE

LOOP-DE-LOOP 49

Life After Near-Death 49

A Simple Question Becomes the Turning Point................ 51

Barbara the Lab Rat...52

The Magic Bullet 53

The Focus of this Book – and What Is Possible 55

The 9 "D's" of De-Looping...................................57

Consistency and Commitment Are Key............................59

Your Mind Is Like a Computer.................................. 60

Your Strange and Magnificent Mind 61

A Powerful Tool Without "How-To" Instructions............62

The Mind Loop Ride 64

Daniel's "Best Friend"...66

Your Spectacular Brain To the Rescue! 67

The Hiking Trail..69

The Miracle of Self-Directed Neuroplasticity....................70

PART FOUR: DE-LOOP WITH THE FIRST

4 STEPS 75

The First "D": *Detect*....................................75

Detect Technique: Spy On Your Thoughts 77

Six Tips To Becoming a Great 007 79

Sound Weird? Try This: 81

This Book Comes Equipped With a Life Preserver! 81

Be a *Scientist*-Spy 82

Specific Mind Loop Phrases To Listen For 83

A Mindfulness "Warm-Up" If You're Having Trouble
   Spying On Your Mind 84

Final Thoughts on Spying On Your Mind 85

The Second "D": *Detach* 86

What "Detaching" From a Mind Loop Will Do For You ... 88

Interruption Technique #1: "My Left Foot" 88

How To Use the "My Left Foot" Technique 90

Interruption Technique #2: "The Name Game" 92

How To Play "The Name Game" 94

You Can Play "The Name Game" By Naming Your
   Emotions Too 95

And... "The Name Game" Works With Physical
   Sensations Too 96

The Third "D": *Detour* 98

Detour List Ideas 99

Make Your Own *Detour* List 100

The Foundation Is Laid 101

The Fourth "D": *De-Story* 103

Stories Are Everywhere 104

We Love Our Stories 106

"War Stories" 107

De-Story Is NOT About Denying That Something

    Happened 108

Six Big Reasons Why De-Story Is So Important 109

How To De-Story 111

What Makes a Great Story? 112

De-Story Methods 115

De-Story Method 1: A Diamond In the Making 115

Your Greatest Teachers, Gifts, and Foes 116

A Love Story 117

If It's Easy, It's a Gift: Drums and the Funny Guy 118

De-Story Your Opponents and Struggles: Discover

    the Gifts 120

De-Story Method 2: The Mystery of Memory 122

Changing Memories *Consciously* 124

De-Story Your Childhood Memories:

    9,460,800 Minutes 125

De-Story Method 3: The Umwelt 127

The "He's Too Cool For School" Guy... And the

    "Happiest Couple In the World!" 128

De-Story Your Memories and Assumptions

    About Other People 130

De-Story Method 4: De-Story to De-Stress 131

It's Not Just the Big Events... 132

It's All Relative... 133

De-Story Your Stress: What a Great Problem

    To Have! 134

Unnecessary Stress: The Case of the Missing

    Thank-You Cards and Green Napkins....................... 134

De-Story Your Stress: We Make the

    Unimportant, Important 135

De-Story Bottom Line 136

PART FIVE: TIPS FOR DE-LOOPING SUCCESS 139

3 Tips To Jumpstart Your De-Looping........................... 140

CONCLUSION..143

You Don't Need To Do This Program *Perfectly*

    To Get the Benefits! 144

Life Is Like A Wave.. 145

To Sum Up the Key Points In This Book:....................... 146

Next Steps 147

Final Thoughts... 150

AFTERWORD 153

Your Two Free Bonuses... 153

Want To Take De-Looping Further? 154

NOTES..159

CREDITS AND ACKNOWLEDGMENTS.................163

ABOUT THE AUTHOR...166

INTRODUCTION:
WHAT'S THIS BOOK ABOUT ANYWAY?

Why You Need To Read This Book

If you've picked up this book, chances are you're in some kind of pain. You may have thoughts in your head that criticize you, depress you, or create stress, anxiety, and overwhelm.

You also may have dreams and goals that keep getting tossed to the wayside because of conscious (or unconscious) fears or self-doubt. Or because that old phrase from a parent or teacher years ago has replayed so many times in your head that it's now your own voice. You know the one:

"You're not good enough." "You can't do it." "You're ugly." "You're not talented." "You're just a screw-up." "It's not going to work out anyway, so why try?"

Maybe you've tried positive thinking, therapy, or any number of other methods to feel better. And while some may have helped, you still find yourself going back again and again to the same self-defeating thoughts, habits, and emotions that make your life miserable.

If you're thinking, "There's *got* to be more to life than this!" You're right. More peace, confidence, and happiness is available to you than you can imagine. It's a matter of getting out of your own way. More specifically, getting your self-limiting *thoughts* out of your way.

You're so much more powerful than you know.

Once you stop the *repetitive, negative thoughts* – what I call "Mind Loops" – your spirit has a chance to breathe again; time expands because you're not spending hours or days (or as in my case an entire *month* once) "looping" over and over on a bad situation until you're drained, depressed, and feel about as big and worthy as a crumb under the kitchen table. Your personality blossoms, you look and feel more refreshed and bright, you smile more often, you have more energy, sleep better, have more creative ideas, get more done, love more, receive more. You *live* more – and *better*.

The question is: "How can one *stop* repetitive, negative thoughts? After all, they're practically on automatic: They're habitual, ingrained and unconscious. The negative statements feel as true and real as 'the sun will come up and go down tomorrow.'"

Since 2010 I've worked hard to answer that question for myself. After a great deal of research and experimentation, I developed a program that freed me from my own repetitive, negative thoughts. This book will show you the exact techniques I used (and continue to use with myself and clients) to stop Mind Loops from hooking me and draining my life of joy.

If you're ready to let go of that kind of mental and emotional suffering and start experiencing more joy in your life, this book will give you tools to do that.

FAQ: For the Curious and the Doubtful

Q: How do I know if I have Mind Loops – and if this book is for me?

Ask yourself these questions:

- Do you doubt yourself – your abilities, your appearance, your decision-making, intelligence, or your future happiness?
- Do you criticize and judge yourself often?
- Do you hold yourself back from going for the goals and dreams that are really important to you?
- Do you say no to parties or opportunities because of social anxiety?
- Do you easily get jealous, compare yourself to others, or feel envious of others' good fortune?
- Do you have body issues?
- Do you worry a lot about the future – or someone else's

future whom you care about?

- Do you replay "movies" in your head of sad or upsetting moments from the past – or of scary possibilities in the future?
- Do you have trouble sleeping – or wake up in the middle of the night full of adrenaline – because of worrisome thoughts?
- Do you hold onto resentments (ie, grudges), or often blame others?
- Do you have self-defeating habits, beliefs or assumptions?
- Are you aware of any inner dialogue that demeans, criticizes, or limits you – especially if it plays over and over in your head?

If you said yes to any of the above, you have Mind Loops.

Q: Is this like psychotherapy?

No – although some aspects of the work were inspired by insights and techniques of some therapeutic models.

No doubt, there are extraordinary benefits from therapy and counseling. After all, it's through self-reflection that we come to know ourselves and to grow. Therapy and Mind Loops techniques are simply two of many paths toward self-growth and happiness, and they can be excellent adjuncts for each other. I've had plenty of therapy myself and much of it helped a lot.

But the Mind Loops system doesn't involve going back in time to delve into the deep, dark past of *where* or *how* Mind Loops started in you. In fact, that type of therapy can sometimes *trigger* a Mind Loop! That's why the 3rd "D" of De-Looping is about shifting your focus *away* from the habitual thoughts that keep you feeling down, and *toward* thoughts and activities that create more happiness in your life.

Also: This isn't a methodology that takes years of unraveling and effort. You can feel better *fast*. And with consistency, you can feel GREAT.

Q: Does this work for clinical depression, obsessive compulsive disorder, etc?

I'm not a doctor nor do I "play one on TV." Clinical depression and obsessive compulsive disorder are medical conditions. Nothing I say should be construed as a substitute for professional medical treatment, diagnosis or advice.

Q: How long does it take to work?

Everyone is different. Most people feel immediate relief when they *Detach* and *Detour* from a loop. Keep in mind however, these are *neural pathways* (literally connections in your brain) you'll be changing, and to do that takes some time, consistency and focus.

Q: Are you a psychologist?

I do not have a Ph.D. What I have is a tremendous passion for self-directed learning (autodidacticism), which supplied me with the stamina and discipline to compile all the research needed to develop a method to stop repetitive, negative thoughts. I also had the personal motivation to do so. (Not to mention a near-death-experience).

Scholarly degrees can be helpful. But so are life lessons. If you have doubts about the power of self-directed learning, this list of autodidacts (plus a few college dropouts) may cause you to think twice:

Benjamin Franklin, Abraham Lincoln, Henry Ford, Bill Gates, Harry Truman, Steve Jobs, Stanley Kubrick, Thomas Edison... and many more.[1]

Q: Will the Mind Loops be gone forever?

The steps and techniques in this book can be used with significant results. I'm a living example of this – as are many of my clients.

We all have "sticky areas" in our personalities that can get emotionally triggered – almost instantly. In those cases, I see more of a *fading* of their intensity. You aren't triggered so quickly or deeply, which gives you the chance to stop the negative thought or emotion from exploding into a full-blown Mind Loop. In other words, you may feel uncomfortable for a time, but you can pull out of it more quickly and the loop doesn't last even remotely as long.

I can tell you with assurance that deep mental grooves *can* and *will* be changed. Whether the Mind Loops disappear altogether... That depends on the person, the depth of their Mind Loops, and how consistently they use these techniques.

(For those that need them, I also offer deeper techniques to pull the more deeply ingrained loops out by their roots. Those techniques are done one-on-one in my Mind Loop Mentoring practice. I have seen deep-rooted shame, low self-esteem, and other debilitating beliefs and feelings virtually *disappear* from clients. It's mind-blowing to watch! But you'll make a *ton* of progress with just the techniques listed in this book).

Q: Is this book going to tell me to "just think positively"?

Nope. This material is based on neuroscience. Affirmations are helpful, but we'll be changing the way your brain is literally *wired*.

Q: Your title mentions a near-death-experience. I don't believe in that stuff and it sounds weird and woo-woo to me.

No problem. I'm not looking to change your world view. My near-death-experience was obviously an incredibly personal and unusual experience in my life. So much so, that it took me four years to "go public" about it. The only reason I'm revealing it now to a wider audience is because of the enormous transformations that occurred as I began "de-looping" my negative thoughts – which were a direct result of that experience.

My story may not match up with your belief system, and that's okay. *Life is a mystery.* Sometimes words cannot describe the indescribable, or make sense of the unexplainable. *This was my experience.* Take what rings true for you, and leave the rest.

Here's the goal: To free your mind of the negative thoughts that are causing pain and suffering in your life. *To bring you peace of mind.* So you can go on to pursue the exciting goals and dreams you have for your life, to have successful relationships, and to live as joyfully as you possibly can. So when you get to the end of your life, you can look back on it not with regret, but with gratitude, fulfillment, and joy.

My Mind Loops Story

Why am I the perfect spokesperson for Mind Loops? Because boy, did I ever have them. (Note the *past-tense*!). Here's a quick rundown of my life story and how *loopy* things got because of them:

I grew up in a family of talented and eccentric artists and musicians. As is often the case with creative people, life was not exactly... "normal." We didn't have much money, and life was often surreal: Rock-n-roll bands in the basement, a brother who'd cite passages from surrealistic treatises as we ate cereal out of those little cardboard boxes, and a Swiss mother trying to create some order out of the chaos. Oh yeah: And then there was the occasional TV flying out of the 2nd story window – just for kicks.

Even with all the craziness, I loved my family – and I adore every one of them now.

I did need to learn a few "survival skills" to navigate the home-life waters however: An over-developed sense of responsibility? Check. How about acutely tuning into the emotional state of the people around me to make sure I didn't "rock the boat?" You bet! These skills served me well then, but as I grew older and didn't need them anymore, many turned into liabilities. I've worked very hard to overcome those old, unhealthy habits.

The last habit I needed to overcome was an unconscious, invisible villain that continually caused havoc in my relationships, devastated my self-esteem, and shackled my most cherished goals and dreams. I had little idea this villain even existed – and *no idea* of the monumental effect it was having on my life.

This villain was Mind Loops.

Over the course of my life, I've accomplished many personal and professional goals, including directing award-winning films and music videos, performing in clubs since age 16 on a variety of instruments, releasing two solo albums, and owning my own film production company. There were quite a few highlights, but one of my personal favorites was the joy of singing and recording with Stone Gossard of Pearl Jam.

I'm proud of my accomplishments. But if you only knew what negative thoughts spun in my head during every one of those experiences, and the uphill battle I was experiencing "behind the scenes" as I waged war with my own mind. I'd swing wildly from confidence to low self-esteem, from boldness to fear and anxiety. I even watched the movie "Gladiator" *13 times* (the equivalent of a 40-hour work week!) in an attempt to catch the spirit of the strong gladiator in my own psyche.

I'm certain my list of accomplishments would have been longer if I'd known about Mind Loops and how to stop them earlier. And I definitely would have *enjoyed* every one of those experiences even more.

So how *specifically* did Mind Loops get in my way?

The Many Sides of Mind Loops

By the time I was 13, I was so shy I could hardly open my mouth to speak to anyone I didn't know well. This social anxiety was hair-raising for me. I can remember a few times I could hardly stand to be in my own body, I felt so out of place and afraid. Of course this meant I had few friends. I might have lived a very lonely and isolated childhood... except I was blessed with the best bestie anyone could wish for – more like a sister – who played with quirky me nearly every day even though she was outgoing and could have had a million friends.

The reason I couldn't speak up is because of the negative thoughts that played over and over in my head: "You're not good enough," "You don't know what you're talking about," "Maybe they're right and you're being an idiot," "You don't have anything interesting to say," "You speak too slowly," "You won't remember your facts"... The list goes on and on.

Although it changed over time, the trouble I had with speaking up stayed with me for years and created innumerable complications when I became an adult:

I failed job interviews because my mind would freeze up and I could barely answer the questions the interviewer was asking me.

I was unable to express my needs clearly which interfered with my relationships (romantic and otherwise).

I'd forget lyrics and even sing off-key (sooo embarrassing!) because anxiety would kick in exactly when I'd set foot onstage to perform.

I had difficulty telling people they'd crossed a boundary with me. So I'd cave in, go silent, feel spacey (somewhat out of body), and observe life almost like I was watching a movie. I wasn't *present* anymore.

I bet most people who have known me over the years would be shocked to know how insecure I felt at times. My "coping mechanism" was just to deny that I felt that way and barge through. I'd *force* myself to do scary things all the time, just so I wouldn't live a boring, isolated life.

That doesn't mean the Mind Loops went away. I just learned to live with them. Somehow.

In addition to my shyness and difficulty speaking up, Mind Loops found other ways to plague me and hold me back. Here are a few examples:

I spent way too much time and energy over-worrying about loved ones – to the point of waking up in the middle of the night in a cold sweat from fearful dreams about the person I was worried about. Mind Loops can create very scary potential scenarios if you listen to them. The majority of those scenarios never happened – and I couldn't have changed the ones that did anyway – so all that worrying didn't help me or anyone else. All it did was take a major stress toll on my health and appearance. (Stress does that!).

I would negatively compare myself with other people – specifically with people who had spent years getting to the level they were – and here I was thinking I should be at that level too, even though I was just a beginner. Voila! Instant feeling of: "I suck."

I would put other people's needs and wishes before my own life and dreams. My Mind Loops told me this was the right thing to do! (*Not!*).

I'd give my power away to other people, which left me with lowered energy, depression (I was on anti-depressants for years), and a big mental nest of confusion. Basically I was trying to live up to what *other people* wanted, instead of loving and accepting myself just how I am. I was looking for "perfection" and guess what? I wasn't that! (No one is). Thank goodness. Being perfect would be terribly boring, wouldn't you agree?

The Turning Point

The turning point occurred during a near-death-experience in 2010. (I describe that mystical, life-changing event in detail in Part 2). During that ordeal, I was "shown" how Mind Loops were pulling the steering wheel of my life toward a ditch. It was one of the most frightening few hours of my life – and yet I wouldn't trade it for anything in the world. Because if it wasn't for that experience, I might never have discovered Mind Loops – nor gotten out from under their spell.

My life is *very* different now! I literally didn't realize that there's a *whole other level* to how wonderful a person can feel. We can't imagine this when we're just living our lives day-to-day. But after a lot of hard work clearing out my negative thinking, I've been able to break through *several levels* of happiness in the past few years. I remember laying in bed thinking, "I can't believe I feel so *good* right now! Life couldn't possibly eclipse *this*!"... And then somehow I'd experience an even *higher* level of joy and connection, health and well-being.

How does this translate into my life?

I absolutely *love* the work I do; it's incredibly fulfilling to me. My relationships are healthy and loving, with depth and meaning. My life purpose is clear. Instead of losing energy and good health with age, I'm in better shape and have more energy than ever before. I feel peaceful and confident. And at last there's a flow of money in my life, which gives me the time and freedom to take adventures and enjoy my days on this earthly plane.

I'm not saying this to boast. I'm saying this because I'm just as surprised at you will be when it happens to you – to discover what's *possible! I simply had no way of imagining that this type of exuberance existed.*

That's not to say that nothing "bad" ever happens! Life always brings its challenges – and I've dealt with some doozies even since my near-death-experience. *But now I have the de-looping tools to not get snagged and pulled down by them.*

Thankfully, you don't have to endure a near-death-experience to get the benefits of mine. In this book I share with you the exact steps I used (and continue to use) in my own life, to shift your negative thinking – so you can start breaking through your own barriers and experience greater confidence, peace of mind, and happiness.

I had a 2nd chance... And now you can, too.

A Summary Of What You'll Get In This Book:

In Part 1, I go into greater detail about what Mind Loops are and why it's worth your time and energy to read this book.

Part 2 tells the strange and harrowing tale of my near-death-experience, and how that led to the whole *concept* of Mind Loops.

In Part 3 we'll dig into the brain science that serves as the foundation of my "9 D's of De-Looping" system – specifically the miracle of "self-directed neuroplasticity."

Part 4 is all about De-Looping! We'll go into detail on the first 4 D's of De-Looping, which is the foundation to release negative thoughts.

In Part 5, I go over 3 Tips for De-Looping Success to help you start your de-looping with clarity and focus.

You also get TWO FREE BONUSES:

A **Mind Loops Workbook** to help you apply everything you've learned to your own life. It's available as a download at http://www.MindLoopsWorkbook.com.

An mp3 audio of **"The Seven-Day Mental Diet: How To Change Your Life In a Week"** by Dr. Emmet Fox (and read by me). It's inspiring, motivational, and the perfect way to begin your Mind Loops Program. Get it at: http://www.7daymentaldietbook.com.

******

I challenge you to keep an open mind, try these techniques out, and do the exercises in the Workbook.

See for yourself how they work in your own life. Once you start to experience the mental serenity and emotional lift that's possible in a life without Mind Loops... I think you'll never go back.

So... Take a deep breath. Are you ready for more confidence, peace, and happiness in your life? If so, it's time to weed out those negative thoughts and start *really living*.

PART ONE:
WHAT ARE MIND LOOPS?

"The greatest discovery of my generation is that man can alter his life simply by altering his attitude of mind."
– William James

"The highest possible stage in moral culture is when we recognize that we ought to control our thoughts."
– Charles Darwin

"A man is but the product of his thoughts. What he thinks, he becomes."
– Mahatma Gandhi

If unhappiness was personified as a dog right now in the United States, it would look like a 6-month-old yellow lab that's been fed caffeine for a week straight, and suddenly let out of its crate into a stimulating pet store. Chaos! Confusion!

Freak out!!!

Unhappiness is running *wild* in the United States.

Just picture this: If you lined up the number of people in the U.S. alone, shoulder to shoulder, who are taking anti-depressants or anti-anxiety medications, you'd see a human wall strung from San Francisco to New York City *and back again.*

Two times.[2] [3]

And that doesn't even include all the people who want medication but can't get it or afford it.

The rest of the world hasn't missed out on this Unhappiness party either. Our human wall of folks from around the world who are suffering from depression would circle the Earth *five times.*[4]

Unhappiness comes in many flavors: Money and health issues, loneliness, regret, uncertainty, worry, stress, and not being able to stop eating, drinking, shopping, or caretaking.

If we added all forms of unhappiness together, our human wall would probably reach the Man on the Moon's nose crater.

What's going on here?

Mind Loops

Jonathan is a successful entrepreneur who lives in a designer home in sunny Tucson with his family. From the outside, it looks like he has everything. And yet, when we began working together, he felt blocked in his life, was on anti-depressants, cringed at the idea of going out of the house, and felt basically unhappy. He described the feeling as "a mysterious force that's holding me back from taking advantage of all life has to offer. It's like an amorphous anxiety. I can't quite put my finger on it, except to say: I would love to feel happy, but something's in the way."

Margo is a successful designer in a great marriage. Yet she's longed to be a musician her whole life. She's composed scads of songs, plays multiple instruments, and studied at high-level academies. But her self-talk is so packed with self-criticism, that only a couple of close friends even knows she plays music. The mere *idea* of sharing her songs – let alone playing live in front of a audience – sends adrenaline rushing through her body. Fear grips her to the point where the idea of "following her passion" was quickly becoming one of life's greatest regrets.

Kendall has a large social group and a booming real estate career. And yet she feels lonely, increasingly tired, and can't keep a relationship going for more than a year. She realized she'd been altering her behavior and choices *based on what she thinks others are thinking about her* ever since she can remember – and it's finally taking its toll. She covers up her real feelings (which are often hidden even from her) with jokes and self-deprecation, and is exhausted from keeping up a persona that's not authentically her.

Brandon is a single lawyer who's a worrying *machine*. He'd like to be in a relationship more than anything – but, as he puts it, the only thing he spends his energy on (besides his stressful job) is worrying endlessly about his aging mother and addicted sister. All he can think about is what he can do to help them. Big dramas never let up in their lives – so dreams for his own life keep getting put onto the back burner.

All of these people are extremely bright, creative, self-reflective, and successful. But lurking just below the conscious mind of each of them like a hyper-efficient virus... is a Mind Loop.

Mind Loops are repetitive, negative thoughts, worries, fears and emotions.

And they're tricky buggers, because they can be difficult to detect. Occasionally you may catch your mind drifting off into that same rotten memory again, or lost in a worry. But most people *aren't aware of what's being said in their own heads*. Their thoughts are just running on their own, like a computer program set to automatic.

If life sometimes feels like you're driving in a car with the brakes on – struggling to find momentum even when things are going relatively well, or else moving forward in dramatic fits and starts – you're witnessing the *effects* of Mind Loops.

Mind Loops Are Sticky and Contagious

We all have negative thoughts from time to time. So I guarantee I won't be telling you to: "Just think positive thoughts all the time!" I've heard people say that and I don't think it's realistic or even necessarily healthy. Negative thoughts are just part of the yin-yang of being human. Every one of us has bad days, we all get our hopes dashed from time to time, and it's healthy to get angry sometimes. But "normal" negative thoughts come... and *go*.

Mind Loops on the other hand, aren't just fleeting negative thoughts; they're the sticky ones, the repetitive ones. They're the ones we *dwell and ruminate* on. Many hide behind the heavy, dark curtain of your subconscious. And they *steal your energy and zest for life* by holding you back from playing music or changing jobs or asking that beautiful person to go out with you or becoming an entrepreneur or asking for a raise or telling someone they've crossed a boundary.

In short, they keep you from getting your needs met and achieving your goals and dreams. And they don't exist in a vacuum either.

Mind Loops are contagious and every loop breeds another. A *cycle* develops, where a negative *thought* triggers a negative *emotion* that leads to a negative *action*.

Sadly, those negative actions *reinforce* the original negative thoughts – and the cycle just spins on and on. Uninterrupted Mind Loops like this can quickly spiral a person down into depression and anxiety.

Mind Loops aren't particular about whose head they squat in either. They infiltrate the minds of both the rich and the poor; young hipsters and seasoned oldsters; famous and unknown, single and married, all cultures, all genders... Basically they're *everywhere*. No one is immune.

Believe me, I've self-reflected over the years until I was blue in the face. I've read hundreds of self-help books. I've tried countless methods including counseling to get past my own mental rubbish. And I quietly took anti-depressants for many years. Most of these things helped me somewhat... but they didn't fix the underlying problem.

If only someone had told me about Mind Loops years ago! If only I'd had a system to help me *erase* and *replace* the corrupted program in my brain! It boggles my mind to think how many painful ordeals I could have avoided, how many low-spirited days I could have bypassed, and how much further I'd be in the things I want to do and accomplish.

But hey – better late than never! And the great thing is that it led me to create the system I had so wanted... for *you*.

How Much Are Mind Loops Running *Your* Life? – Take the Quiz

The following questions paint a picture of how Mind Loops can secretly infiltrate your thoughts and life. How many would you answer *YES* to?

DO YOU...

- have career ambitions, relationship desires, fitness/energy goals or other longings that somehow seem to elude you and you can't figure out why?

- spend a lot of time thinking about the past, or the future?

- have thoughts, worries, or inner dialogue that repeat over and over in your head like a bad song?

- have an inner voice that berates, criticizes or judges you? (ie, "That was a stupid thing to do!" "You're so fat." "You can't do that." "You're too old.")

- often think questions that have no real answer? Such as:

  - *"What if* I don't ever meet someone to fall in love with?"
  - *"Why* did this happen to me?"
  - *"How come* I was born with this ailment / these parents / this problem?"
  - *"Why* do I have such bad luck?"

- rerun movies in your head that create scary or disturbing scenarios of what *could* happen with a particular situation?

- feel anxious, sad, angry, depressed, jealous, resentful, confused, disappointed or afraid more often than you'd like?

- overanalyze situations – weighing the pros and cons, going through scenarios of: "If I do X, then Y might happen, in which case I'll do Z..." And yet rarely does all that overanalyzing and wheel-spinning result in an actual plan of *action*?

- often view your life through *gray*-colored lenses (instead of the rosy-colored kind)?

- engage in revenge fantasies?

- sometimes make yourself "small," or feel like you could be living a "bigger" life?

- when you receive a compliment, say to yourself: "They're just trying to make me feel good, they don't really mean it."

- find that you can't stop thinking about a breakup and all the memories and emotions that invokes?

- hear yourself saying, "You can't do that," or "You aren't good enough" when you start moving forward on a goal you want to achieve?

- when things are going well, tell yourself: "Uh oh...! This means something bad's going to happen any second now! Things are flowing too well!"

- have a hard time asking for help – or accepting help when it's offered?

- finally make a decision to lose weight, stop smoking, or any other lifestyle change, and a voice in your head keeps sidetracking your momentum by saying, "Nah, you can start that *tomorrow*."

- feel a disconcerting *pleasure* when you replay a memory of a past event that made you furious or sad? Or have a strange *impulse* to worry about an event in the future?

- feel *stuck* in one or more area(s) of your life?

- have trouble finding the "off" switch once you start thinking a negative thought?

If you said yes to three or more of these, then Mind Loops have nudged their way too far into your driver's seat.

If this all feels a little overwhelming right now, just know that pretty much everyone suffers to some degree with this rubbish going on in their heads. We try to hide it. We don't want to admit we ever think nasty things about ourselves, have fears, insecurities, worries, anxieties. But I guarantee you're *far* from alone in this...

You're In Good Company

You probably know *intellectually* that other people deal with Mind Loops – or at least you suspect that might be the case. But to have *proof* that's true is another thing altogether, and it can make you feel, well... better.

So I compiled some surprising comments from names you'll definitely recognize just so it's *crystal clear* you're not alone with your Mind Loops.

These people are gorgeous, extremely successful, and working in careers many would die for. And yet when you read their comments you'll probably think, "WTF?" Because they reveal their Mind Loops, their hidden negative thoughts – things you'd never in a million years guess were going on in their heads:

"I struggle with low self-esteem all the time. I have so much wrong with me, it's unbelievable."
– Angelina Jolie

"You think, 'Why would anyone want to see me again in a movie?' And I don't know how to act anyway, so why am I doing this?'" – Meryl Streep

"I have self-doubt. I have insecurity. I have fear of failure." – Kobe Bryant

"I still doubt myself every single day. What people believe is my self-confidence is actually my reaction to fear." – Will Smith

"I have a fantastically loud and mostly punitive voice in my head that says, 'You're not good enough, you stink.'"
– Emma Thompson

"I think my biggest flaw is my insecurity. I'm terribly

insecure. I'm plagued with insecurities 24/7."
– Madonna

"I'm really insecure about everything. I never think I'm worthy of anything." – Megan Fox

"I was constantly attacking myself: 'You're a fake, you're a fraud.'" – Robert Pattinson

"As a teenager I was so insecure... And my self-image still isn't that alright. No matter how famous I am, no matter how many people go to see my movies, I still have the idea that I'm that pale no-hoper that I used to be. A pale no-hoper that happens to be... a little lucky now. Tomorrow it'll be all over, then I'll have to go back to selling pens again." – Johnny Depp

"I'm always described as 'cocksure' or 'with a swagger', and that bears no resemblance to who I feel like inside. I feel plagued by insecurity." – Ben Affleck

"I doubt myself 400,000 times per 10-minute interval."
– Taylor Swift

Surprise! As you can see, you're in good company.

Mind Loops are everywhere. But what's really exciting is that you're taking conscious action to change your loops. It's time to take your mind and life *back!*

You CAN.

> *"Only I can change my life. No one else can do it for me."* – Carol Burnett

> *"The only person you are destined to become is the person you decide to be."*
> – Ralph Waldo Emerson

The Techniques outlined in this book are extremely effective. They work. You'll feel better – and relatively quickly.

Not only that, but I'll be breaking down the process into clear steps that will be easy to follow. And the techniques themselves are thankfully *simple.*

Your job? *To work with the steps as consistently as possible.* The longer you stick with it, the deeper and more lasting the transformation.

Remember: Changing habits can be difficult for anyone, and you're going to be changing thinking habits you've had for years – probably since childhood. Think how long you've been unconsciously reinforcing those negative thoughts!

With this program, y*ou'll be literally reconfiguring neural pathways in your brain.* So give the techniques – and yourself – a chance to work. Make a decision now to commit to really working with these steps. That kind of commitment is the first step to changing everything.

I know you CAN do this because I've seen it happen again and again.

And also for this reason: YOU picked up this book. That tells me a lot. Not everyone is willing to spend time and energy on themselves to make their life happier. Not everyone is willing to step out of their comfort zones (no matter how harmful they are) to change. *But you are.* That tells me you have an intention to *grow*. And I want to applaud and honor you for that!

Can't Wait To De-Loop?

If you're lost in a loop right now and want relief *pronto*, feel free to skip ahead to the two Interruption Techniques listed under "The Second "D": Detach" in Part Four.

Keep in mind however: Interrupting a loop is just *one* piece of this de-looping puzzle – it's not the whole shebang. Adding in the other steps and techniques is what's really going to drive out the loop. But it will help tide you over as you continue reading the rest of this book.

Just remember: Interrupt, rinse, and <u>REPEAT</u>! (Translation: *keep interrupting your loop* every time your thoughts return to that dark place). This takes conscious intention and awareness... but the relief will make your efforts worth it.

Open the Parachute

"Your mind is like a parachute. It only works if it is open." – Anthony J. D'Angelo

A note about the material in this book:

There will be some people who will reading along and at some point roll their eyes and think, "Oh, not *that* again! I already know that."

Yeah. I get it. While a lot of this material is new, some of it you may already be acquainted with. I *expect* that. But what is familiar to you may be new to other people and vice versa.

I also expect it for another reason. I know that voice. It's the part of our brains I call Godzilla. Godzilla's the one who serves up Mind Loops as easily as he spews fire-breathing bad breath, and he loooves to tell you: "Skim over this. Tune out. I know that already!"

Whenever Godzilla rears his annoying fake plastic head in your brain, instead of giving in, ask yourself, "Okay Godzilla, simmer down. Even if I have heard this before, what *new angle* can I take on this?"

Because I *guarantee* you're a different person now than when you heard it the first time: *300 million* sweet cells in your body kick the bucket *every minute* – and are instantly replaced by fresh cells. And with each new thought and experience, those new cells start behaving differently... and that includes your thoughts. So give those ripe, little new cells an interesting angle to chew on.

Life is more interesting when our minds are *open* and creative than closed and stuffy with stale air, right? Let's open the window (and the mental parachute) and let some fresh ideas flow.

And by the way, that "new angle" might actually be how you can *apply* the concept of what you're reading to your life. So often we know what will make us feel better – but we don't do it. Maybe you needed to hear it this time so it would stick.

You. Are. Great... Period.

> *"When I let go of what I am, I become what I might be."* – Lao Tzu

> *"It is never too late to be what you might have been."* – George Eliot

Deep down you know you have greatness. You know you're capable of creating, contributing, receiving, and *being* more than you are now. And certainly being *happier* than you are right now. Isn't that right?

The thing is, it's very hard for happiness to coexist with repetitive negative thoughts. But when you change your thoughts, you transform. You'll look and feel lighter. You'll start attracting people into your life who lift you up instead of put your down. You'll get more done because you won't be wasting time looping on situations you can't control, or on grievances from the past.

If you don't take care of your Mind Loops now – in the form of self-doubt, worry, stress, anxiety and depression – you'll be robbed of living as full a life as possible during this precious time you have on earth.

So congratulations for picking up this book. You've taken the first step toward experiencing that sublime and sometimes elusive state we call: Happiness.

PART TWO:

MY NEAR-DEATH JOURNEY

T he leaves from a luxurious Cottonwood tree flickered in the breeze above my head. Sunlight drifted through the branches, spotting my eyes. In the distance I could hear the reverberating voice of a lecture taking place in a huge tent. I was laying on the soft ground in the middle of nowhere, a remote area on Vancouver Island. It would have been a sublime scene... Except for the fact I was dying.

How on earth did this happen... To *me?!*

Just months earlier I was onstage, singing with Stone Gossard of Pearl Jam before a cheering crowd. That part of my life was going well. I had the best musical partner and friend I could ever wish for... and I was getting paid to do what I loved to do: Music.

And yet "behind the scenes" my life was a nest of problems. I was going through a divorce, I still wasn't earning enough money to make ends meet, and worst of all, my self-esteem was unreliable. It would shift wildly from high to low and back again. And during those low moments it had as many holes as Charlie Brown's Halloween ghost costume. But even with quite a bit of therapy under my belt, I still couldn't *see* those holes – let alone know how to patch them up.

Until one particular evening.

I was on tour with Stone. While singing and dancing onstage, my focus suddenly turned to one particular fellow in the front of the audience. The reason he caught my eye wasn't because he was so hot or charismatic or because his smile was so big. It was because his arms were crossed and his expression was one of defiant disinterest in our performance. I could have ignored him and focused on the rest of the audience who *was* engaged in the show.

But no. I started thinking, "Why doesn't that guy like our music? Why is he standing in the front?... Do we suck tonight? Am I singing off-key? Oh shit, here comes that high note again... I'm probably going to miss it! Then he's *really* going to frown!"

On and on my inner dialogue chattered *while I continued to sing, dance, and perform.* It was disconcerting to be so ultra aware of my Outer Life (singing, remembering lyrics, interacting with the band and audience) *while at the same time* being ultra aware of my Inner Life (thought after thought after thought, the majority of which was fear-based).

It was a defining moment for me because it was the first time I had "tuned into" my thoughts with such detail and clarity – and it was disturbing to say the least.

When I laid in bed that night, I pondered this strange experience and wondered: "Is that the kind of thing my mind is saying *all* the time? Thoughts full of fear, self-doubt, comparisons and a slew of "Why's?"

I remembered that just before we went onstage, Stone was complimenting me on my singing and had suggested it was high time I start singing solo. He knew I composed my own music. "Why not start rolling out your own tunes? You're ready. In fact, you're overdue."

I deeply appreciated his confidence in me and my talent. But the thought of going out on my own made my hair stand on end.

As I laid in bed that night, I thought about the level of anxiety his comment brought up in me. It forced me to wonder: "Where did this lack of confidence come from anyway? Is it valid? I had already done a *ton* of gutsy things in my life... So why do I feel so timid?"

And then that inner dialogue returned: "Are you kidding, Barbara?! You don't sing that well! Not only that, but you'd be tongue-tied in front of an audience. You really want to reveal yourself through your music? Give me a break. And you'd have to organize a band! What the hell are you *thinking?!*" I wanted to yell "Shut up!" but it was my own mind hounding me. I couldn't get away.

It was at that moment I decided I needed to make a change. Did I want to keep playing small – or did I want to reach my highest potential?

That's when the Anaïs Nin quote I'd always loved came back into my thoughts:

"And the day came when the risk to remain tight in a bud was more painful than the risk it took to blossom."

Immediately I jumped out of bed, did an online search for one of those camps that push your boundaries and help you develop courage. I found one... and signed up. I went to bed excited about the adventure that awaited me.

A "Premonition"

The evening before I was to leave for the camp, I was just finishing my packing when an intensely disconcerting feeling began to build.

I suddenly felt sick to my stomach. Immense doubts and fears about the camp bloomed like an unexpected crop of invasive weeds. Was this just same ol' Fear dropping in for another visit? Or was this Intuition? The sensations grew so intense, I considered canceling... if it weren't for the fact that my closest friend Michele had agreed to sign on for the camp too. I'd be letting her down if I bowed out now. I had to go.

And yet... My mind kept saying these ominous words:

"Your life will NEVER be the same after this camp. Savor your life as it is right now, because you WILL be different. Life will dramatically change after this. Good luck and 'sweet dreams'!"

I rolled my eyes at my sarcastic and dramatic mind. "What

do you mean 'sweet dreams'? You think I can sleep now, after hearing all *that*?!"

I tossed and turned all night.

The next morning I met Michele at the train station. As we boarded, I said a silent goodbye to my current life as I knew it. I didn't breathe a word to Michele about what had transpired the night before. We took our seats, and the journey began.

Intensity

The first thing the camp had us do when we arrived was to sign a liability waiver. A big, long, scary one. It basically said: "I understand I may be injured, maimed, paralyzed, or even die at this event. I agree to not hold [the company] liable for any misfortunes that befall me during my attendance this week."

Michele and I raised our eyebrows at each other and hesitated, our pens poised above the signature line. But what were we going to do? Go home?! We had just taken a car, train, bus, and cab to get to this remote place.

We signed and went off to set up our tents.

Every day at the camp we faced a new fear. I can't actually divulge the challenges they put in front of us since I signed a non-disclosure contract as well. But I can tell you we faced fears involving heights, fire, scary people, and some other things I won't even hint at because you'd think I was insane for even agreeing to them. I slept just 3 hours a night for a week. I sweated more than I have in my life (and showered just once –

for less than 5 minutes), and I ate mounds and mounds of food and yet still lost weight from the exertion.

Did I develop courage? Most definitely. Did I increase my confidence? Absolutely. Was I scared shitless? Yes, often. Was I glad I came? Even with some mixed feelings, my answer would be: No doubt about it.

Then came the final main day. I was scheduled to do an endurance challenge. I ate a humongous breakfast as usual and got ready for whatever the day would bring. We were put into teams of two. I was matched with a delightful young woman from Mexico City who was nervous about the event, so she asked me to be in front and lead the way. I was happy to do so.

Off we went. It started out great... The day was sunny, the scenery gorgeous. But halfway through the event I started to feel... *funny*. I noticed my vision shifting in a way I can only describe as "sparkly." I grew weak – and quickly. I slowed down, even had to sit down to regain my strength. I thought perhaps I was dehydrated, even though I'd been drinking plenty of water. I drank more anyway and stayed on top of it just in case. My young teammate grew concerned about me, but I acted as though everything was just fine – I didn't want to worry her. But after my 3rd request to sit down and rest, I finally confessed I wasn't feeling that well and put her in front.

The longer we went, the more strange the world appeared to me. Sounds now had an echoey quality to them... When my teammate spoke to me, her voice sounded like it was coming from yards away, while conversations far in the distance sounded close. I felt so weak and shaky I was afraid I would collapse on the spot. But the whole challenge was based on a *group* of us returning; I couldn't let them all down! So I kept gulping water and somehow pushed on.

At last we saw the finish line up ahead. As we drew nearer, people were lined up on both sides cheering us on. What I then saw disturbed me more than anything else had so far: The people on the sidelines were *strobing*, like some chilling special effect from a horror movie. The cheers were reverberating and slowing down and warping. Flashes of light would invade the scene and the sparkles in and around everything grew to an alarming degree.

Now I was certain: Something was *definitely* wrong.

Once through the finish line, I grabbed an acquaintance and whispered, "Please get one of the guides, I think I'm going to faint." He agreed nonchalantly and sauntered off to find someone as I sat on the ground, alone. Minutes passed... I felt my heart rate shifting, and all of my senses continuing to distort everything I saw and heard. I was having trouble breathing. Time crept on as I tried to hang on. "Where the hell is my friend?!" I thought.

Finally he returned – alone. "They said to just sit down, that you'd be fine," and he walked away.

I looked around me. My world no longer resembled anything I had seen before. It was one giant, surreal light and sound show, and I felt so alone.

*****

"The boundaries which divide Life from Death
are at best shadowy and vague. Who shall say
where the one ends, and where the other
begins?" – Edgar Allan Poe

*****

Somehow I made it back to the camp. I asked around until I found a medic. Or perhaps I should say a "medic" in quotes. I think the most medical training this sweet fellow had under his belt was a 3-hour Red Cross CPR class. And yet, he was the best they had to offer me. I knew I was in trouble when I approached him saying I needed help, and he took one look at my face and his jaw dropped. I think he looked more terrified than I did.

Quickly he sat me down and gave me a drink with electrolytes. He took my pulse and blood pressure and with each test he turned more and more pale.

My friend Michele strolled up to me smiling. We hadn't seen each other all day and she had no idea what was happening to me. She said, "There you are! I've been looking all over for... Oh my God, *what happened?*"

Only later did Michele describe my appearance: My skin was gray as dust, and the hugest dark circles underlined my vague, confused eyes as if I'd stayed up every night since puberty.

Quickly Michele and the "medic" began discussing what to

do. It was decided that I'd go lie down in my tent. It was a far distance away however and by now I could barely walk. So the "medic" said he'd be right back with some vehicle.

He returned with the strangest car. It was small like a golf cart – but it had this odd ability to run right over just about *anything*. He pointed the vehicle in the direction of my tent and we drove straight there – "as the crow flies" as they say – over bushes and rocks and anything in our path that wasn't a tree. It just added to the surrealism of my dream-like existence.

The sun had transformed my tent into a sauna, so they set up my sleeping bag underneath that magnificent Cottonwood. The "medic" said he'd come check in on me from time to time, and he took off.

The next 5 hours were some of the most intense of my life. Michele sat quietly beside me the entire time, doing Reiki, giving me sips of water every so often, and praying.

The Terror Begins

"Michele! My leg! My left leg!"

"What is it Barbara? What's going on?!" Michele asked as calmly as possible – although I could hear the fear in her voice.

I was panicking because I could *feel* the sensation in my left leg diminishing, draining away... until my leg was completely numb.

Then it was my right leg. Then both of my arms. One by

one, my limbs were "disappearing"...

Until I became just a torso and a head.

Have you ever cried so hard that you had a hard time believing your body was even *capable* of producing so many tears? I've no newbie at crying, but this was altogether different. These were tears from the depth of my being. I was terrified.

And it was in this state of terror and helplessness that the movies began.

The Teaching Begins

A "movie" started playing in my head. It was a scene of me with my brother from just a few months prior. The movie was shown in perfect clarity and detail, not like some fuzzy memory. I heard the sounds, I saw minute and specific expressions.

At one point, the movie froze into a still frame. And I heard "Someone" – a neutral inner voice – ask, *"What did you mean when you said that to your brother?"*

My crying slowed down. I didn't stop to consider what was going on or who was doing the asking. I just thought about the question, and answered it – out loud, as far as I know.

As soon as I answered, the screen was cleared and a new movie began.

The next little movie was of me onstage the night I became so focused on that fellow in the front row with his arms crossed. A slew of still frames were fired off to me from that night, always ending with the same question, *"What were you thinking right then?"*

Next up was a scene between my ex-boyfriend and I during a band rehearsal gone badly awry.

Again the movie still-framed and I heard, *"You wanted to say something right at this moment, but you held back. What did you want to say?"* I remembered the chaos of the moment, and the disturbing mixture of emotions I had been feeling: Anger, judgment, sadness, compassion – and that I just wanted to get the hell out of there. But instead I stayed and didn't say anything. As time went on, I quietly withdrew more and more until I was a shell of who I am.

I told the voice what I had wanted to say and this time I got a follow-up question: *"Why didn't you?"*

For some reason this question had never even entered my mind – that I *could* have said something! I was stumped and very surprised at myself. Perplexed, I just said, "I don't know," and the movie wiped off the "screen" and another movie began.

On and on, movies, still frames, and memories from my past came up. Over and over I was asked questions:

- What was I thinking at that moment?
- What did that reaction mean?
- Did I say what I truly wanted to say?
- What was my body language saying – with a raised eyebrow, a pivot of the head, eyes turning down, or a

deep sigh – in response to a comment or situation?

There were several times that I answered the questions with what I thought was the *right* thing to say – to look "good" so to speak. (*Who* I was "looking good" for exactly, is beyond me). This wasn't a conscious decision on my part – and oh how I appreciated being caught in the act! Whoever this voice was knew the Truth, and I wasn't going to get away with trying to fool it with some self-righteous, goody-goody answer. This was full-on humility and owning up to my own thoughts, feelings, and actions. Whenever I heard the follow-up question: "Are you *sure* that's what you were thinking?" or "Is that *really* what you wanted to say?", I was forced to dig deeper and ask myself: "Hmm... *Is* that what I was thinking?" I discovered I'd been deceiving my *self* at times; and gradually I started to see the patterns lurking beneath my habitual thoughts and reactions.

I believe this was a Life Review of sorts. A very specific analysis of my thoughts and behaviors across my life. And this Life Review continued for literally 4 *hours*.

The entire time, the questioning was calm and steady. It was emotionally neutral – or at least non-judgmental. And the only thing it was after was pure HONESTY and TRUTH.

The Question That Altered My Life Forever

At last the questioning came to an end.

All throughout this process of watching the movies, answering questions and the Life Review, my body continued its downward spiral. It was like I was skirting the edges of two different worlds: Slowly I was occupying that "other realm" more and more – while less of me was here, in the physical reality we call "life."

It was at this point that things took a turn for the worse, physically: I literally *felt* my spirit leaving out the top of my head. I could feel my energy and life force draining out of me.

Tears came fast and furious. I knew how serious the situation was. I remember yelling out to my dear friend beside me, "Michele! I'm dying! I'm dying! I feel my life force seeping out! It's leaving from the top of my head!"

I have no idea how Michele responded. My eyes were closed and any words she said sounded miles away. I just sensed her calm and loving presence nearby.

Then out of the blue... An unexpected calm flooded into me.

The same "voice" returned and asked me the most important question of all: "Barbara, you have a choice to make now. Do you want to stay? Or do you want to go?"

I knew exactly what I was being asked. Did I want to stay in my body and continue my life? Or did I want to exit and go... wherever that may be?

Oddly enough, I didn't automatically jump at the chance to continue living. Why? Because what I felt on the other side was so welcoming, so loving, and so indescribably peaceful. I could sense: No more struggle, no more striving, no more...

But then I thought about all of my unfinished projects. What about *them*?

Now it was *my* turn to ask some questions.

"Well... If I decide to *go*, what'll happen to my music? My projects? My unfinished albums? What about all of my writings? They're not done yet!"

The answer delivered a big dose of benevolent humility:

"Barbara, your projects, your albums, your writing, your *work* is not what matters the most. What does matter... are your *relationships*. How you treat others, how honest you can be, how much you show your true self, how much you can *love*... and how much you love *yourself*. If your music moves people, connects you to them, or them to others or more deeply to themselves, then yes, your projects are important. But what really matters are the connections you make between yourself and others."

I was stunned. I sighed. I felt relieved and sad at the same time. And *confused*! If I chose to go back to my life... What the hell was I going to do?

As I took everything in, it suddenly made all the sense in the world to me. From this perspective, I understood life was about *connection*. How connected are we with others? Do we avoid connecting? How deep are the connections? Do we truly *care* about others? How honest and *real* can we actually be? And if we're not really connecting with ourselves and others, *what is it that's getting in the way?*

My life force continued to seep out of the top of my head. Sounds grew fainter. The sunlight I had been sensing through my closed eyelids grew dimmer. I knew time was running out to make a decision.

"If I decide to go back to my life, is there anything in particular I need to do?" I asked.

"Yes," I heard. "There are certain people you need to see. You need to tell them how much you love them. Even if you think they already know it, you need to express the depth of your love to them. Tell them *why* they matter to you, what their presence in your life has meant and given to you."

The voice then told me exactly which people in my life I needed to say this to.

"It's time, Barbara. What is your answer?"

One direction – strangely enough, deciding to *go* – led to warmth and ease.

The other direction – staying – led to uncertainty. But it also led to the opportunity to express love, and heal broken relationships. And to continue the strange adventure that is Life. I made my decision.

"I'm ready. I'd like to stay."

The moment I made the decision, my energy started coming back into my body again: Sensation began to return to all four of my limbs. I felt calm and at peace.

For a few minutes I laid there quietly, experiencing the sensation of limbs and life again. I heard clapping in the distance from within the lecture tent – and the disturbing reverb on sounds was quickly fading; it just sounded like clapping again.

Slowly I opened my eyes. The first thing I saw was Michele sitting beside me, holding my hand and deep in prayer. The sun was now low and orange, and creating exquisite patterns on the ground as it glinted through the leaves.

I watched the bushes as they gracefully danced in the breeze. I saw Michele's auburn hair gleam, and a bee buzz gently nearby.

I was back.

PART THREE:

HOW TO GET OFF THE NEGATIVE LOOP-DE-LOOP AND BACK INTO HEALTH AND HAPPINESS

Life After Near-Death

"Life is better than death I believe, if only because it's less boring, and because it has fresh peaches in it." – Alice Walker

After my near-death-experience, the entire next month of my life was beyond *extraordinary*. Every moment of every day was exquisite and blessed. *I was high on life.*

I remember one morning I woke up from a bad dream. It was a dream that usually would have down-colored my mood for the entire day. I started going down that same well-worn path when it dawned on me: "Wait a minute! I'm *alive!* I got to experience a bad dream! How cool is that?! What a trippy experience, what a fascinating dream!" And I sprung out of bed, excited that I got to experience that bad dream!

My relationship with music also shifted. As I continued to sing, I noticed how lyrics I had sung many times before now somehow contained extra meaning that I hadn't noticed. It felt like I was "downloading" the emotions behind the lyrics, which made singing them even more meaningful and stimulating.

My own musical "spigot" was flowing like never before as well: A friend came to stay with me shortly after my near-death-experience. Right in the middle of our conversations I'd suddenly jump up and exclaim, "Oh! A song is coming! Be right back!" and I'd rush into another room with a recorder and sing an entire song – the music, lyrics, and arrangement all wrapped up and ready to go. I ended up releasing a 2nd solo album with that material.

And I distinctly remember the experience of simply eating a peach. I sat down on my red couch with the most voluptuous peach on my plate. For a long while I just gazed in admiration at the multitude of reds, oranges, and yellows of this peach. I then "petted" it's soft fuzz, marveling at the texture. I sliced off a chunk with my knife and watched as the juice spilled out, a sensual sweet scent wafting into the air. I brought that slice of perfect fruit to my nose and could not believe the fragrance up close, and full.

It was as though the scent and structure of the peach were encompassing my whole being at that moment. Every sense was engaged. As much as I'd loved peaches in the past, I felt I'd never truly experienced a peach before!

I licked the juice and was blown away by the sweetness, the sunshine, the life force I could literally *taste*. It was an experience akin to ecstasy.

I spent the next 40 minutes eating that unbelievable piece of fruit. I was completely present and feeling overwhelming appreciation – not just for the peach itself, but for the ability to eat and for the sensation of taste and smell.

We eat while watching TV without even a thought. We gobble things as quickly as possible – in the car, while working at our computers, as we rush out the door – not realizing it's truly one of the greatest sensations on earth. Not to mention the smell of food, or how it feels against our fingers.

This peach incident was such an incredible high. If I ate like that all the time, sure, it would take longer, but the enjoyment factor would go through the roof. I wondered, "Could I sustain this kind of conscious presence all day, every day?"

A Simple Question Becomes the Turning Point

For me, the answer to that question was: Nope. At least not to that degree.

Ever-so-slowly, the high from my gratitude for just being alive began to wear off. I started to catch myself eating more quickly, or forgetting to *notice* the diversity of trees and colors around me, or to smell the fragrance of the air while on a walk. And yes, sometimes a bad dream *did* downturn my day.

Other tendencies started creeping back in as well: Self

doubt, comparing myself to others, over-worrying about loved ones, and self-criticism. Little by little, negative thoughts and behaviors were slowly re-emerging.

Until one day, I finally asked myself a simple question:*"What was the common denominator of all those hours of questions I was asked during my near-death-experience?"*

That was the turning point.

Because it dawned on me that the line of questioning was all about my *thoughts*. What type of *thought* was behind every reaction, gesture, emotion, or behavior during each scene I was shown in that "life review"?

The answer hit me like a ton of bricks: *Negative* thoughts. Self-limiting thoughts. Thoughts that made me and my life smaller instead of grander. *But I hadn't been aware of them.* All those years... It was a sobering, humbling moment.

And motivating.

That's when I began my research to find the most powerful, quickest, easiest, and *lasting* methods to heal the damaging habit of repetitive, negative thinking: Mind Loops.

Barbara the Lab Rat

"You want experimentation. Every once in a while, you stumble upon something that blows your mind." – Jeremy Stoppelman

In my quest to crack the Mind Loop code, I began an intensive study of how the brain works, aspects of psychology and the subconscious, even how our *cells* deal with thoughts and emotions. I attended more classes, seminars, lectures and workshops, meetings, counseling/therapy sessions and consumed more books, interviews, documentaries, audio and video programs and podcasts – than I can count. All the while working with my own intuition and Higher Power to test out every technique I could find.

Some worked well for me, but I never found the "magic bullet". So, without realizing it, I began to design a custom program to heal myself of the Mind Loops I had suffered from all my life.

The Magic Bullet

The results have been nothing short of extraordinary: I absolutely love my life. I experience flow almost every day. What I can only describe as miracles happen to me so often that sometimes I feel like I dropped into Jeannie's magic bottle: Opportunities appear in bizarre and wonderful ways... Money flows into my life... I'm healthier and definitely *happier* than I've ever been.

So much happier in fact, that after years of taking anti-depressants, I'm thrilled to report I was able to successfully stop taking them three years ago! And I continue to feel as happy as a monkey with a peanut machine.

Do I still get Mind Loops? Sure. Life is full of new challenges every day. And we all have specific loops that are stickier or deeper than others. The same goes for me.

The difference is, now I know what to *do* with a Mind Loop. I don't get stuck there long. Often I can laugh things off, where before I couldn't even see a hint of humor. Everything's smoother now. Easier. Funnier. And the world responds differently to me as a result.

As far as the big issues go, they've shifted so dramatically in my life that even the high-octane ones have lost so much of their steam, I can't even remember why they used to cause me so much grief.

Can you imagine? For just a moment, think of an awful memory or worry you tend to dwell on that always shifts your mood into sadness or anger or fear. Now imagine that it has *lost all of its power*. The *charge* is gone. Sound impossible? It's not. De-looping is truly extraordinary.

Through my research, direct personal experience, and lots of trial and error, I developed a *specific, powerful system* to de-loop Mind Loops, and then re-program the mind with supportive new beliefs and thoughts. I call this system, "The 9 D's of De-Looping." It serves as the basis for all my programs as well as with clients in my Mind Loop Mentoring Program. It's my "magic bullet."

The Focus of this Book – and What Is Possible

"Once you replace negative thoughts with positive ones, you'll start having positive results." – Willie Nelson

My goal is to give you the tools to blast through the blocks that have been holding you back (possibly for years) and get you feeling better *fast*. <u>So we'll be focusing on the first 4 "D's of De-Looping."</u>

The process of becoming unbound by the negative thoughts that hold us hostage is not a straight line. There will be ups and downs, twists and turns. But if you make a consistent effort, the road will always be moving upward.

<u>If you will commit to following these four steps consistently, you *will* feel better</u>.

Everybody is different, so the timing and specifics of what you can expect will vary. But here are markers you may start noticing along the way that will show you your life is indeed transforming.

Little by little (and sometimes in great bursts) you will:

- discover parts of yourself that were missing or inconsistent before: Your power, your confidence, your ability to bounce back, your compassion, and your sense of worth
- experience more humor in life – and in yourself
- notice that people are responding differently to you –

more smiles, more connection – because you'll be emitting a very different expression of who you are

- feel more capable to meet life's challenges – so much so, that the idea of pushing your boundaries to move toward your own dreams and potential will be exciting (even if still a little scary)

- instead of over-worrying or negative obsessive thinking, you'll feel more acceptance of *how things are* and be able to let things go more easily

- feel more self-worth... so the desire to take better care of your body, keep tabs on your stress level, and accept help from others will come more naturally

- be more able to forgive... and thus develop more love, tolerance, and compassion for others

- not care so much about what other people think of you

- roll with the punches more at work and home instead of allowing others to ruin your day

- experience less drama and overwhelm... so you'll begin to know the meaning of peace and balance

- diminish your judgment and criticism of other people... so you'll experience more love and joy in your personal interactions

- discover there are people and things worth trusting – including yourself

- naturally start seeking out new experiences and friends who support and encourage you instead of bringing you down

- feel more appreciation for the small things and more gratitude in general.

I realize these may be hard to believe right now. But I know what this program can do. *Life is better de-looped.* WAY better. And it all begins with the first four "D's".

The 9 "D's" of De-Looping

The 9 "D's" are broken down into 3 phases:

Phase 1: De-Looping Mind Loops
Phase 2: De-Looping Negative Emotions
Phase 3: Re-Programming

As I mentioned, in this book we'll be focusing on the first phase, De-Looping Mind Loops, because it's *foundational* to feeling better.

De-looping basically means you'll be "deprogramming" the negative messages about yourself that you've acquired over the years. These false messages have been heard, thought, and/or spoken so many times that they've become part of your belief system. Deprogramming them takes time, energy and *consistency.* But if your mind isn't *de*-programmed, you can't *re*-program it – and that's when life *really* starts cooking.

Here is an overview of the first four steps in "The 9 D's of De-Looping":

1) **Detect** – What thoughts are you actually saying in your head? *Who the heck knows?* Our thinking can become so habitual and automatic that many, if not most, of your loops can slip under your conscious radar. So how do you detect unconscious thoughts? The 1st "D" helps you tune into what's being said in your head, and just under your conscious awareness.

2) **Detach** – When we're stuck in a worry or a negative thought or emotion, it's like we're "one" with the Loop. We can't see it as simply another opinion, belief, or feeling; it has grown over us like moss until we're one giant Mind Loop topiary. The 2nd "D" gives you powerful methods to *separate* yourself from the negative thought or emotion. The Mind Loop simply becomes a thought – nothing more, nothing less.

3) **Detour** – Shifting your focus and thoughts *away* from the Mind Loop is critical. This is much easier said than done, however. Mind Loops are as sticky as an old diner menu – and they can pop back into your mind before you have a chance to say "basket of fries." This "D" gives you tips about the most effective ways to create space between you and your Loop du jour.

4) **De-Story** – Are memories set in stone? Are opinions *facts*? Many Mind Loops are created when we inadvertently mistake our *interpretations* of

experiences for *facts* – or ruminate on specific memories that color the overall experience gray. This "D" is like the pull-cord on your mental parachute. You'll be able to see painful situations from broader and more supportive angles so some fresh air can enter into old, stagnant points of view.

Consistency and Commitment Are Key

The de-looping process is similar to a food detox, where you remove dairy or wheat or whatever is causing the allergic reaction in your body. But in this case, you're removing toxic *thoughts*.

Why is that important?

Because as long as we continue to put ourselves down, tell ourselves we can't do something, or how nothing ever works out for us, our lives remain small and struggling. We never reach our real potential. Our health, sleep, energy, aspirations and joy of living can't get a foothold.

As long as we continue judging, comparing, criticizing and resenting other people, we'll never have the love and supportive connection we crave.

Removing your toxic thoughts is *imperative* to experiencing real happiness, peace, and confidence.

And like with any detox, consistency and commitment are key: Observing your thoughts and taking action *right away* with the tools I'll be sharing with you, is essential to interrupt any Mind Loop before it gets a chance to hook you and pull you down.

As you become aware of your loops and start to interrupt them, you'll be literally plugging up energy leakages in your body, mind, and spirit. You start feeling better because you'll be reallocating this energy toward things that nourish your spirit, heart and relationships, your self esteem, and your physical health.

The addictive or obsessive feeling you may experience when you're looping will also diminish. Because there's *literally* a cellular, biological addiction going on that makes you crave the brain chemistry behind your Mind Loops.

Your Mind Is Like a Computer

"I regard the brain as a computer which will stop working when its components fail."
– Stephen Hawking

Have you ever gotten a virus on your computer? What a *drag*. Suddenly none of your programs run smoothly, and emails are sent to your contacts that falsely *appear* to be sent from you – when in fact the virus will be in charge (and yes emails from the virus will often be nasty and bizarre). The computer will slow down – and sometimes crash. And the virus can even damage memory.

Sounds like a Mind Loop to me.

If your mind is a computer, Mind Loops are like viruses installed on the hardware of your subconscious mind. As long as the viruses are there, you're not going to function properly. You won't act "like yourself" with others, you'll get overly tired, and sometimes you'll crash. Your memory will diminish from stress, and your negative outlook will actually *change* your memories and perceptions.

You can add as many new software programs as you want, but until you remove the computer viruses – the Mind Loops – you're not going to fulfill those deep, luscious goals you feel you were born to do... Nor feel all the excitement and happiness that life has to offer you.

The first 4 D's will remove the Mind Loops virus from your mind's computer.

Let's dive in.

Your Strange and Magnificent Mind

Pop Question #1: How many thoughts would you guess you think each and every day?

10,000? That seems like a lot of thoughts... But it's more.

40,000? Nope. Higher.

The answer is: *You think approximately 60,000 thoughts every day.*[5]

Sixty-thousand thoughts! What would your life be like if even *half* of those thoughts were brilliant and supported you?

Thankfully *some* are. But here's where things get strange.

Pop Question #2: How many of those 60,000 thoughts would you guess are repeat thoughts? Where you're thinking the same thing, again and again and again?

The answer is: *A whopping 90% of your thoughts are repeats*, according to the latest scientific research.[6]

Repeat thoughts aren't *all* bad; they have their value and place in our lives. Repetition helps us learn facts, figures, names. It's also key to making affirmations work, and it's critical to changing habits and developing new skills.

The real problem is this: *70% of all of our thoughts, for most people, every day... are negative.*[7]

Seventy-percent. No wonder we have problems!

Just imagine if you had a spouse, parent or boss who absolutely believed in you, was a fan of your work, and always had words of support and love for you. Don't you think you would perform better in your life, feel good about yourself, and get through the hard times with more ease?

Now imagine if all that support and love was constantly running *in your head;* that loving spouse, parent or boss was *you.* How do you think that could benefit your life?

The truth is, if you change even *10%* of those 70% of negative, repetitive thoughts, your whole life would transform.

A Powerful Tool Without "How-To" Instructions

"Mind: A beautiful servant, a dangerous master." – Osho

We're given this *extraordinarily* powerful tool called our mind. But we aren't taught how to *use* this tool. It's like handing kerosene and matches to a child. Unless we know how to direct our minds, we can do tremendous harm to ourselves.

One of the truly odd things about your mind when you stop to think about it is: *It's always ON.* It's like a machine with no Off switch. You wake up in the morning and within *seconds*, it's back on, going all over the place:

> "Oh no, I have to talk to Shirley about that stupid project today. Why are they having me do that project anyway? Just a waste of everyone's time. I can't stand my job. I just want to stay in bed. I was having such a great dream. What was it again? Man, they disappear fast. ...What is a dream anyway? They're so weird. Okay, get up. Gotta brush your teeth. Oh yeah – I gotta make that appointment with my dentist. We'll see if my insurance pays. Probably won't. 'Cause they suck. Huh. Wonder if my dentist is back to work yet, or if he's still on that long-ass vacation? Why can't *I* go on a vacation? 'Cause I can't afford to go anywhere, that's why! How am I ever going to be able to quit this damn job?!"

Sound familiar? Your mind is *constantly* at work. It's either processing information like you're doing now as you read this, or remembering something from the past, trying to keep track of what you're supposed to do tomorrow, or fantasizing about the future, worrying, complaining, desiring, or analyzing.

When we get into negative habits of thinking, into *looping*, the reason it's so incredibly destructive is because, unless you're a master meditator, *there's no turning off the machine*. And that's how we end up repeating *thousands* of negative thoughts every day.

The Mind Loop Ride

"I have a tendency to sabotage relationships; I have a tendency to sabotage everything. Fear of success, fear of failure, fear of being afraid. Useless, good-for-nothing thoughts." – Michael Bublé

Have your thoughts ever felt obsessive or even addictive in a way? Where your mind is running rampant, taking you on some painful ride and you don't know how to get off? That's the Mind Loop ride. It includes:

1) <u>Attacks on self worth</u>. These loops may cut you down, criticize you, question your talents, blame you for things you didn't even do, cause you to worry about everyone to the point where you put their needs first and stop taking care of yourself and your own needs. Sometimes you may even (mostly unconsciously) stop yourself from succeeding because you're worried it might hurt someone else if you "surpass" them in some way. Mind Loops shrink your life, joy, and potential.

2) <u>Your physical health is also *deeply* affected by Mind Loops</u>. Because thoughts and their associated emotions *literally* change the biochemistry of your body.

Author and neuroscience researcher, Dr. Joe Dispenza, in his book, <u>You Are the Placebo</u> states: "When we focus on thoughts about bitter past memories or dreadful futures... we're turning on the stress response *by thought alone.* If we turn it on and then can't turn it off [because we're looping], we're surely headed for an illness or disease – a cold or cancer – as more and more genes get down-regulated." [8]

Mind Loops that trigger anger, disappointment, resentments, regret and other intense emotions can be so painful that we'll attempt to erase and deny them with as much force as we can muster because sometimes that's the only way we can handle the pain. This kind of denial is actually an important survival mechanism that can provide *short term* relief.

Those negative emotions don't just go away because we forced them off into a dark corner though. Not by a long shot. In fact, we pay dearly for ignoring them.

Stem cell biologist Dr. Bruce Lipton, and neuroscientist Candace Pert, Ph. D, have both shown that suppressing emotions interrupts the normal functioning of cells at a molecular level, which can increase the risk of illness. It's as though we're bathing our cells in a soup of toxic chemicals.

Dr. Lipton puts it this way: "Almost every major illness that people acquire has been linked to chronic stress."[9]

3) On top of all that, <u>every time you engage in a Mind Loop,</u> <u>there's a _leakage of your life energy_</u> that creates dullness, irritability, and fatigue... and can make you feel like you're an abbreviated piece of nothing.

Basically, Mind Loops can become a nasty combination of heckler, persecutor, unfair judge, energy vampire, and goon all rolled up into one big bully.

But you can't just run away from the bully or avoid it − because the bully lives right there in your own mind.

Daniel's "Best Friend"

A smart and talented client named Daniel contacted me after a job interview that revealed to him just how much his Mind Loops were undermining him.

Daniel had loved his position at a software start-up... until the company folded and he lost his job. He's someone who enjoys working hard and contributing, so being unemployed became extremely uncomfortable for him.

He diligently searched for jobs and finally there was an opening for a fantastic position at a company he was excited about. After a phone interview, they were eager to meet him in person. Excited, he prepared intensively for the interview, and even bought a new shirt.

The interview went well and he went home with high hopes. Two days later he got a call from the company. They said, "Thanks for interviewing with us. But we're going to pass.

Good luck with your search."

He was shocked, and just sat there in disbelief. Finally he called his best friend for moral support. After hearing the story, his friend said, "Well, I'm not surprised. I don't even know why you thought you could land that position in the first place. Come on, you're not *that* smart. Get realistic. You'd be better off going for more of an entry level position."

What kind of friend would say that to him when he was already knocked down?!

No real friend would. Because it wasn't his friend saying those nasty comments: *It was his own mind.*

The Mind Loop bully strikes again.

Your Spectacular Brain To the Rescue!

Thankfully your brain is spectacularly designed to help you out. Big time. And most people don't know their minds can do these "magical" things, or how to develop the skills to *access* their mind's unique talents.

Neuroscience is giving us an unprecedented understanding about how our brains work – and how we can literally, *physically* change our thoughts.

When you're in the middle of a problem, what do you spend most of your time thinking about?

Did you answer, "I'm thinking about how to solve the problem... *of course!*"

Our impulse is to analyze what's happening (or happened),

and how to solve it. That's a natural response.

But if you look deeper at this "analysis" of the problem, you might find that you're thinking a lot about what you *don't* want to happen. We think about all the scary possibilities in the future, how unfair someone was, how hurt we feel, or how "stupid" we were. We overanalyze, try to figure it out, how we should respond, and attempt to answer the question: "Why is this happening to me?!"

What neuroscience tells us is:

Wherever you put your attention and focus, the brain responds by *prioritizing* and creating *new circuits* there.

So if you're focusing on what you *don't* want to happen – the worry that wakes you up at 2am, the memory that makes you so mad you're grinding your teeth to stubs, or the disappointment that stops you in your tracks and makes you reconsider your lifelong dreams – you're not only *firing up* your brain circuits around that issue, you're *fortifying* them more than ever.

The key is to *interrupt* the negative Mind Loops. Interrupt the neural, electrical charge that's focused on the problem, on what you *don't* want. Then shift your attention instead onto things you *do* want.

The way you do that, the way you *rewire* your brain, is by changing your "neural pathways." Neural pathways are literally electrical pathways in the brain, similar to the electrical wiring in a house. The more you repeat and focus on something, the stronger the pathway gets.

Sound impossible to rewire your own brain? It's not. Read on!

The Hiking Trail

> *"As a single footstep will not make a path on the earth, so a single thought will not make a pathway in the mind. To make a deep physical path, we walk again and again. <u>To make a deep mental path, we must think over and over the kind of thoughts we wish to dominate our lives</u>."*
> – Henry David Thoreau

One way to understand neural pathways and how they work is to imagine you're going for your usual hike in the woods. You know the trail, you've been down it hundreds of times before. It's clear and easy to walk on. That hiking trail is like one of your well-worn neural pathways – perhaps a negative thought that you tend to loop on for hours and days on end.

Now imagine that today, just before you start down your trail, you look to your right and see a vast wilderness without a trail yet. It intrigues you... So you decide to check it out – but there's no trail there yet. So you start bushwhacking through the foliage and moving logs to create a new path.

As you explore this new part of the woods, you suddenly come upon a stunning field of wildflowers! Wow! They make you happy, so you decide to come back the next day.

When you return the next day, you can see the start of the rough trail you bushwhacked through the day before. You take that route again, and as you make your way to that stunning field of wildflowers, <u>you're making your new trail even more solid and real</u>.

This area is so beautiful that you start hiking this new trail every day; it's more fun even than the original trail. *And here's the magic*: As you continue taking your new path, the *original* (Mind Loops) trail slowly grows over with foliage, spider webs and fallen logs because you're not taking it anymore... Eventually it's completely overgrown. At the same time, your *new* (healthier, happier) trail grows clearer and stronger with use.

The Miracle of Self-Directed Neuroplasticity

"Any man could, if he were so inclined, be the sculptor of his own brain."
– Santiago Ramón y Cajal (the "father" of modern neuroscience)

Here's how the hiking trail analogy works in your life, and relates to Mind Loops:

If you're constantly saying to yourself, "I can't do this," you're *physically* solidifying those specific neural pathways in your brain and *turning them into Mind Loops*. You're trudging along that same first hiking trail again and again, making those thoughts clearer and stronger and more "true" with every step, every repetition.

That's when our lives go downhill – because what you think in your head, is reflected back to you in your life.

Let's say you wanted to be an actor ever since you were a kid. But sadly your dreams weren't supported. Instead, you received comments like:

"You? An actor? Get real. Go to college and get a *real* job."

"Hahaha! Acting? Imagine what your ugly nose would look on the big screen!"

"You can't even remember to take out the garbage. What makes you think you could memorize a *script*?"

Now you've internalized those comments and "I could never be a good actor" is the resulting unconscious Mind Loop.

And yet... You still have this dream to act. So you think about joining an acting class. You read the description and it excites you. But then that same old loop starts up (the first hiking trail) and suddenly you're imaging how you'll forget your lines, how stupid you'll look, how people will secretly make fun of your nose, and pretty soon you're being laughed off the stage.

Every time you try to take a step out of your comfort zone toward this goal, the thought, "I could never be a good actor" pops into your head. You feel like you've lost the battle before you've even begun – like something's sabotaging you. Something *is* sabotaging you. It's your Mind Loops.

But these neural pathways can *literally* be replaced by a

process called *self-directed neuroplasticity*. This is what it's called when you replace your existing "hiking trails" with the new ones that you've consciously chosen.

When you do that, *everything* changes.

Neuroplasticity is a normal brain function that's happening all the time. It's the general process of how neural pathways in your brain (positive *or* negative) are formed in the first place. So neuroplasticity is a physical process that can help or harm you... It all depends on what you're focusing your attention on.

"Those of us who went to school 20 or 30 years ago were taught that the brain is hardwired, meaning that by the time we're adults, we have a certain number of brain cells that are arranged in fixed patterns or neural circuits, and that as we get older, we lose some of those circuits," says Dr. Joe Dispenza. "We thought that we would inevitably turn out like our parents in many ways, because we could only use the same neural patterns that we genetically inherited from them.

"Neuroscientists now say that was a mistake. The great news is, *each of us is a work in progress*, throughout our life. Thanks to functional brain scanning technology, we can now see that our every thought and experience causes our brain cells, or neurons, to connect and disconnect in ever-changing patterns and sequences. In fact, we have a natural ability called neuroplasticity, which means that as we learn new knowledge and have new experiences, we can develop new networks, and *literally change our mind*."[10]

When you *self-direct* this part of your brain and actively

choose what you want to focus on, extraordinary things begin to occur. And that's what you'll be learning to do in this book. You'll be physically *changing your brain circuits* to reprioritize the thoughts and actions that support you.

It's what the whole De-Looping process is about.

PART FOUR:

DE-LOOP WITH THE FIRST 4 STEPS: DETECT, DETACH, DETOUR, AND DE-STORY

The First "D": *Detect*

> *"I need one of those baby monitors from my subconscious to my consciousness so I can know what the hell I'm really thinking about."*
> – Steven Wright

D*ETECT* is all about becoming aware of what your mind is saying. After so many years of thinking in particular ways, with our specific beliefs (most of which we never chose in the first place), our thoughts have become *habitual*. We become deaf to the smack our inner voice is talking to us and about us. We have no clue we're even looping.

We do notice how crappy we're feeling though. How we wake up at 3am with that same Big Worry night after night.

How we grow silent or our shoulders start aching and our creativity has dried up to a slow hiss. Before we know it, someone's pointing out that we've been wearing that ratty old "Life Sucks!" T-shirt every day for a week.

When life becomes a struggle, sometimes that's our only indication that we've been stuck in a loop, and didn't realize it.

Wouldn't you like to be warned of this mounting storm in advance? You can't do anything about your Mind Loops if they're hidden from you – and many of them are. That's why we start with *Detect* – and why it's of *paramount* importance. If we aren't aware of what needs to be changed, there's no chance of changing it.

What you may discover is that you *think* you know what kinds of thoughts are taking up residence inside your head. But as you consciously put your awareness on your thoughts, you might find out something quite different is going on up there than you expected.

One of my clients, Jeffrey, had a sales job that was based on commissions. He was a self-described "depressed guy" who had taken on a job that required a perpetually upbeat, persuasive persona to sell high-ticket items to potential customers. Not surprisingly, he didn't like his job.

When he started to *detect* what was going on in his head, he discovered his distaste for the job ran much deeper than he thought.

Jeffrey realized that he said the phrase, "I *hate* my job!" 12 times on an average day; that he drifted off to sleep ruminating on that same thought; and was even waking up in the middle of the night in a surge of adrenaline thinking about all the reasons he dreaded his work.

Thinking that bleak thought before sleep and in the middle of the night was especially significant because looping before and during sleep actually deepens the level of one's depression.[11]

Sadly, the more Jeffrey looped, the more he attracted exactly the kinds of experiences he *didn't* want into his life:

Demoralizing interactions with co-workers that reinforced his already low self-esteem. Unimpressed (and non-buying) customers. Less confidence, less motivation to do a good job... And a displeased and now-cranky boss who never wasted an opportunity to let him know it.

Is it any surprise then that Jeffrey's commissions dwindled, and the unemployment office began to seem more inviting than going to work?

How did Jeffrey start turning this situation around? He began by diligently working the first technique: *Spy On Your Thoughts.*

Detect Technique: Spy On Your Thoughts

> *"Until you make the unconscious conscious, it will direct your life and you will call it fate."*
> – C.G. Jung

Whether you're the new 007, Sherlock Holmes, or Columbo, you've just been given a mission: To listen in on the private whisperings of someone who coincidentally looks just like you.

What is s/he saying "behind your back?" About you, or about other people? Sneak up on this person (yes, it's your own mind we're talking about), and listen in – *for one entire week.*

This is an odd and unnatural experience at first. After all, you're spying on your own *mind.*

Pretty soon you'll be glad you're doing it, because you'll start to discover your blind spots. "Blind spots" are the thoughts and beliefs going on in your mind that you have little or no awareness of. The reason you're blind to them is because on some level *you've already accepted them as reality.*

For example, if you have a deep-seated belief that says, "I'm someone who always has bad luck," then it's easy to become *unaware* of thoughts that support it because that belief has become *part of your identity.*

The moment you start observing your thoughts, you're literally stepping *outside* of your "programming." And that's the first step to *changing* the program.

Dr. Daniel Amen, clinical neuroscientist and medical director of the Amen Clinic for Behavioral Medicine says, "Becoming aware of circular or looping thoughts is *essential* to gaining control over them."[12]

Spying on your mind is about noticing what inner dialogue is happening, what thoughts are passing through your head *as they're occurring.* It's like a radio station that you set your mind to listen to. You may be astonished to find out what thoughts automatically pop into your head throughout the day.

Your goals for Spying On Your Mind are:

1) To become conscious of unconscious negative thoughts;

2) To catch a negative thought before it turns into a loop.

You may have heard people in recovery from alcoholism say, "I'll be fine as long as I just don't take that first drink." Mind Loops are similar in their addictive quality: A loop can only get started if you "take" that first negative thought.

When you tune into your negative thoughts, you have the choice to accept them – or to interrupt them, using the steps we'll cover in this book. This is KEY to changing your neural pathways.

So how do you spy on your mind?

Six Tips To Becoming a Great 007

Spying on your mind isn't a *passive* experience that you "accidentally" fall into; it's an *action* that takes conscious choice to do. Here are 5 suggestions to help you pass spy school with flying colors:

1) **Set an intention** to be aware of the first thought that comes to your mind when you wake up. "Setting an

intention" simply means to make a clear declaration to yourself. Repeat it several times, with purpose and meaning. Your subconscious will hear you and help you out.

2) **Set several alerts** on your phone at random times of the day to remind yourself to notice what you're thinking at that precise moment.

3) **Notice** what thoughts are going through your head **as you have a conversation** with a partner, friend, or family member. (Ps: these can be very revealing!).

4) **Emotions** can be like an alarm that goes off, alerting you to the fact that a Mind Loop has been triggered. So if you find yourself suddenly in a bad mood, ask yourself this question: **"What *thought* was I thinking *right before* I started to feel this way?"**

5) **Pretend you're a real SPY!** You just happen to be spying on yourself. Make a game out of it. Get *into* playing the role of a spy. What is your mind whispering to you? Listen in. What is it doing behind your back? Get stealthy. Sneak up on it and find out.

6) *Important*: Like any good spy, as you listen in, take notes. **Write down the thoughts you hear the most in a small notebook or on your phone.** And keep track of *how many times you repeat a Mind Loop* by making a mark beside the phrase in your notebook whenever you repeat it. Your worst Mind Loop offenders will soon start to materialize before your eyes.

Sound Weird? Try This:

I realize that the idea of Spying On Your Mind can seem strange or awkward. But really, you're just cultivating a new kind of awareness about yourself. You may have heard this called "*mindfulness.*" What does that mean exactly?

"Mindfulness is awareness that arises through paying attention, on purpose, in the present moment, non-judgmentally," says Jon Kabat-Zinn, author and Professor of Medicine Emeritus at the University of Massachusetts Medical School. "It's about knowing what is on your mind."[13]

Let's do a quick mindfulness demo right now.

As you're reading this and absorbing the information, simply become aware of the fact that you're sitting there *reading*. There's the part of you that's reading and processing the words, and there's the part of you that can observe yourself doing that. You can switch your perspective back and forth or even do them at the same time.

Weird, huh? Pretty cool, too.

As you spy on your mind this week, instead of just accepting everything your mind says, you'll be *switching your perspective* to *observe* yourself thinking.

This Book Comes Equipped With a Life Preserver!

There's a chance that spying on your mind will bring up thoughts or feelings you'd rather not look at. You may find out you're harder on yourself than you expected, more critical, more judgmental, and sometimes even flat-out cruel. You may discover you're not as loving toward yourself (or those around you) as you thought, or that you're not as kind and magnanimous a person as you hoped you were. And you may be very surprised at just how *much* you loop.

Just keep in mind that this is the first step in *letting them go*.

And you won't be left stranded in the pool of your murky Mind Loops without a life preserver. The 2nd and 3rd "D's" will shift the negative thoughts you find.

In the meantime, one way to make Spying On Your Mind more palatable and less emotionally charged, is to invite in The Scientist.

Be a *Scientist*-Spy

When a scientist is conducting a study, what's the #1 quality they need to make sure their findings are unbiased? Neutrality. They can't *want* the study to go any specific way, or try to squelch the results because they don't like what they're seeing. They must remain neutral and open in order to find the real answers. And that's the kind of spy you want to be.

Whatever you find, do your best not to judge the thought *nor* push it away. Both of these responses are common when we detect thoughts we don't like.

Instead, take the scientist route: Be *curious*. Try not to take the information personally. Just *observe* the activities of your mind, like an eyewitness. And take notes of your findings.

Specific Mind Loop Phrases To Listen For

Keep a close watch for the following phrases:

- "I'm not good enough."
- "I *should* have done" or "I *shouldn't* have done..." or "I *should* be further in my career."
- "I'm not as good /smart / attractive/ confident / talented / thin / young / rich /sexy/ popular or (fill in the blank) as so-and-so." (Anything comparison-oriented).
- "He/she/they don't like me."
- "I don't deserve it."
- "I'll make a fool out of myself."
- "Things never work out for me anyway, so why even try?"
- "I can start this de-looping process (or fitness program or any goal) *tomorrow*."
- "I can't" or "I don't know how to (fill in the blank)."
- "I hate myself" or "I hate my life" or "I hate (anything – fill in the blank)."

If you find any of these loops, stop and take a moment to celebrate your success! You've just uncovered thoughts or beliefs that are blocking you from having the kind of life that knocks your socks off. These loops were *silently* sabotaging your life before. Now they're out in the open. And we're going to start de-looping them out.

An Important Point: If you come across a thought that's particularly stressful, or one that triggers a distressing memory for you, remember this:

"Look... But don't stare!"

Instead of dwelling on it, quickly move to the next two "D's" (see below). Don't allow your discovery of these Mind Loops to send you into another spiral.

A Mindfulness "Warm-Up" If You're Having Trouble Spying On Your Mind

This first "D", Detect, is *vital* to de-looping your negative thoughts. So if you're having trouble spying on your mind, here is a "'warm-up" that'll take less than 30 seconds to do. It'll help you develop that new muscle of mindfulness.

This warm-up purposely doesn't have anything to do with your thoughts. Starting with something other than your thoughts can be a good way to get the hang of this.

The key is just to *notice* what you're doing at any given moment. So right now:

- *Notice*: Are you holding your breath?
- *Notice*: Are the muscles in your shoulders or stomach or any other part of your body tense? (If so, try releasing them. How does it feel?).
- *Notice*: Are your legs crossed? Are you tapping your foot? What is your posture like? Did you just clear your throat?

Practice noticing these simple things for several days. It can be fascinating to start catching your own ticks and habits! Whether it's how you inhabit your body or your mind... It can be a real eye-opening experience.

Once this is easy for you to do, move onto spying on your mind.

Final Thoughts on Spying On Your Mind

> *"The scariest thought in the world is that someday I'll wake up and realize I've been sleepwalking through my life: under-appreciating the people I love, making the same hurtful mistakes over and over, a slave to neuroses, fear, and the habitual."*
> – George Saunders

The *Spying On Your Mind* technique will bring into the light of day specific Mind Loops that have been hiding out in the shadow of your habitual thinking. Because up to this point, they've been largely unconscious – so you've been unable to identify what's been holding you back in a big way.

Your goal is to become aware of *specific phrases* from your inner dialogue. In particular, look out for self-criticism, worries, self-doubt, unreasonable rules and expectations of yourself, gossip, comparison, or judgments of others... Basically any thoughts that are negative, unsupportive, and repetitive.

Mind Loops can be *tricky*. Sometimes I'll catch myself daydreaming: I'll be lying in bed after my alarm has gone off, when suddenly it dawns on me I was lost in thought. I look at the clock... and am shocked to discover a full *30 minutes* has gone by! What on earth was I daydreaming about for so long?

Often it's a *Mind Loop*. I'll be so lost in it, I won't even realize I was ruminating on a past drama, or fantasizing about some future event that may never even happen. What a waste of my time!

Detecting Mind Loops is a skill, just like any other. But I promise you that the more you practice *Detecting*, the faster you'll be able to de-loop them.

Which leads us to the second "D" of De-Looping... Detach.

The Second "D": *Detach*

Imagine stepping onto an elevator, and while riding up to the 6th floor, you suddenly find yourself humming along to the elevator version of a song you can't stand. With a groan, you step out, wondering how long that little gem will be stuck with you. Days...?

I'm sure you could name songs or ad jingles that make you want to kick the TV or audio player out the window when you hear them because you just *know* they're going to stick in your head like a broken record.

Those "ear worms" are a type of Mind Loop in musical form. And you've probably already discovered that just *willing* them to go away doesn't work. Why?

Well... You know the phrase: "What you resist, persists"? Resisting a Mind Loop, or trying to force it to stop, or push it away by willpower alone, will never do the job. In fact that makes it worse.

To stop musical ear worms, you need to *interrupt* and then *replace* the song in your head with one you like.

And that's exactly what you're going to do with the negative thoughts and loops you discovered while spying on your mind.

The 2nd "D," *Detach*, is the "interrupt" part of that equation; the 3rd "D," *Detour,* is the part where you replace them.

The goal of *Detach* is to <u>separate yourself from the negative thought so it becomes just another *thought*</u>. Not a fact, not a reality, not the almighty Truth about who you are. Just a thought. You and the thought are no longer "one." That takes away the bulk of its power and intensity immediately.

What "Detaching" From a Mind Loop Will Do For You

Detaching will:

- bring immediate relief! Take a nice, deep breath because you're about to get a break from the repetition of your negative thought-loop.
- free you from automatic reactions! No more trigger finger! You'll be creating a "wedge" between you and the loop so you'll have a moment to THINK: "How do I want to *respond*?" – versus just *reacting* to a situation. It will give you back your power to choose.
- keep you from falling into the black hole of a full-blown Mind Loop.
- set you on the road to "self-directed neuroplasticity." You'll be hopping off that same old "hiking trail" so you can take a moment to think about your Next Move.

So are you ready to start Detaching? I have two powerful Interruption Techniques for you.

Interruption Technique #1: "My Left Foot"

> *"Only one thing has to change for us to know happiness in our lives: where we focus our attention."* – Greg Anderson

I developed this technique based on an insightful passage by Alejandro Junger, a brilliant doctor who specializes in food detoxes.

We're going to practice this technique right now so you get a feel for it. Then I'll describe WHY it works to help interrupt Mind Loops.

Right now, as you're reading this, put some attention on your left foot. You don't need to look at it; just feel it. Is it warm, cold? Cramped in a shoe or is it comfortable? Feel each toe touching the other one(s)... Feel the texture of your sock or whatever is touching it.

Taking your awareness to an even deeper level, see if you can even feel your left foot... from the *inside-out*. Yep, I know that sounds odd. But try sensing what's happening *inside* your foot, such as the blood flowing through your veins. (It's fine if you don't sense anything, but just play with the idea).

As you keep some attention on your left foot, think about this interesting thought: Your foot was sitting there *before* you put your attention on it. But you weren't aware of it. You only became aware of your foot when you began to *focus* on it.

Which means: Whatever we place our attention on becomes our focus, our experience at that moment. And as Dr. Junger put it, "The total experience of your life is the sum total of every one of those moments."

Focus again on your foot. I don't know about you, but mine starts to feel *tingly* when I put my attention on it.

Why do you think that might be? There may be several

reasons, but the one I want to point out is: When you put your attention on your foot, a whole set of neurons that connect your brain to your foot just *fired off*. Literally, electricity started shooting down into your foot, whereas just a moment earlier, that cable of neurons was idle and quiet. You actually reallocated and *moved* energy, *electricity,* from wherever it was being used before, to your foot.

This energy is by *default*, by automatic *habit*, going into your thoughts.

Most of our thoughts are either focused on memories of the *past,* or fantasies of the *future*. Of course, none of those things are actually happening to you right now. The simple act of putting your attention on your foot *immediately* pulls you back into the *present* moment. Your thoughts have no choice but to simmer down. They're not being fed all that electricity and energy anymore because you used your *will* to shift your focus back onto what you're actually experiencing right now.

How To Use the "My Left Foot" Technique

This week, when you discover a Mind Loop or a negative thought:

1)   If it's new to you and you haven't written it down before, quickly write it down, because that's the main goal of this *Detect* week – to become aware of your thoughts.

2)   *Right away, shift your attention to your left foot.* (Note:

You don't have to specifically use your left foot; you can focus on any body part you want). *Get into* the details of how your foot feels. Feel it from the inside out, as best you can. Focus on it for just 10 seconds or so, then go on with your day.

You may be surprised at how effectively this simple shift of your awareness – away from your thoughts and into your body – can interrupt a Mind Loop.

The negative thought may not be forgotten, but you aren't feeding it anymore. It loses some of its power and you can now focus on something else.

If your negative loop attempts to jump back in and grab your attention again, calmly shift your focus back onto your left foot. Or mix it up and focus on your right foot this time. The point is to keep interrupting that thought as many times as necessary until you're free of it.

Years ago I was a dog trainer, and sometimes Mind Loops remind me of misbehaving dogs! If you've ever had a dog that begged for food at the table, you've probably discovered that the key to stopping the behavior was to ignore them. They'll keep up the begging for a while – and often the behavior gets even worse before it gets better. But if you hold fast and just keep ignoring them, they'll eventually grow tired of the game and give up.

The "My Left Foot" Technique works in a similar way. Mind Loops may "beg" for your attention as you work to re-train your brain. But if you keep ignoring the negative thoughts –

moving your attention away from them and onto your body instead – eventually your Mind Loops will get the message and "behave."

Interruption Technique #2: "The Name Game"

To interrupt a Mind Loop with the "The Name Game" is very simple:

The moment you become aware of a negative thought, or feel an unwanted emotion rising up... *Name* it.

Think back to a time you knitted your eyebrows worrying so much about a family member's health, or an upcoming test, job interview or performance, that you could have made a sweater out of all that knitting. In addition to the crossbow on your forehead, what happened to your mood, your thoughts, emotions, behaviors – even to your body?

When you loop with worry, you're living in the future in your mind. Your imagination starts toying with worst-case-scenarios. The fear and anxiety this worry produces can penetrate your body and spirit in such a way that it feels like it's all happening *right now*.

And here's the secret: <u>*Your body doesn't know the difference*</u>. The chemical cocktail that's being released into your system by your brain at this moment would be appropriate and *necessary* if you were actually in a dangerous, fight-or-flight situation. But you're not.

Instead, the anxious thoughts you're focusing on are *lying* to your brain and body about what's actually happening to you right now. As your system floods with adrenaline, fear and anxiety take hold even more. You may start to get light-headed from shallow breathing. Your shoulder muscles tighten into little cement blocks. Your eyes focus downward, and not even your favorite food placed right in front of you could bring back your appetite. Life contracts and everything feels like it's caving in on you.

Like putting on a pair of ugly dark goggles on a sunny day, the worry *colors your present moment* in an anxiety-ridden, gray hue. You and the worry, for the moment, are *one*.

Time to call on The Name Game for help.

When you harness the power of The Name Game, you pull yourself away from the worry. You're no longer trapped inside the *feeling* of worry. You are you, and the worry is something outside of you. The Name Game allows you to look at your loop *as an objective thing.*

When you separate yourself from a worry – or any other negative thought you're stewing on – you suddenly come back into the present moment. As the adrenaline slows and your breathing gets back on-track, more blood flows into your brain so you can think more clearly, problem-solve more effectively, and make better decisions. You begin to release the stress in your body and breathe deeply again. Your eyes move up, and as you look around, suddenly you remember there's a whole world going on around you.

How To Play "The Name Game"

1) First, catch yourself in the act of looping; *detect* the negative thought or emotion.

2) Give the negative loop a *NAME*.

Examples:

> "That thought is just a *Worry*."
>
> "I'm *Daydreaming* again."
>
> "This is *Negative Thinking*."
>
> "That's a *Mind Loop*."
>
> "That was *Then*, this is *Now*."
>
> "This is my old *Hiking Trail* again. It doesn't lead where I want to go."

Coming up with ludicrous or comical names can kick in the very healthy added bonus of helping you find humor in yourself or the situation:

Examples:

> "Sad Sack is back!"
>
> "Voodoo Voice!"
>
> "Mind Loop brain fart!"

When you *name* the loop, you *detach* from it.

You Can Play "The Name Game" By Naming Your Emotions Too

Negative *thoughts* can trigger negative *emotions*. But sometimes it's easier to detect the emotion than the thought that caused it. In that case, just name the *emotion*.

Examples:

> "This is what *Shame* feels like."
> "I'm *Fear-Looping*."
> "This is *Anxiety*" – or *Depression, Doubt, Disappointment, Frustration, Anger* – whatever emotion you're experiencing.

A fascinating study was done at UCLA, led by Matthew Lieberman, Ph.D, that showed how and why The Name Game works so effectively with emotions – from the angle of what's actually going on in your brain.

The amygdala is the part of the brain that lights up when we're afraid, angry, sad, or stressed out. Using brain imagery, Lieberman and his team found that when test subjects *named* an emotion, the amygdala actually *calmed down*. The part of your brain that triggers negative emotions literally stopped firing so hard![14]

Bottom line: When you play "The Name Game," you can breathe again, your emotional reactions are more in line with what's actually going on... and you can detach from the loop.

And... "The Name Game" Works With Physical Sensations Too

Every emotion creates a physical response in your body. So even if you can't identify the negative thought that's looping in your mind, and you don't know what emotion you're feeling... You'll definitely notice its physical counterpart in a stress headache, tight shoulders or a stomach that suddenly feels sick as a d-o-g.

To play the Name Game here, all you do is *name the physical sensations you're having.*

This simple act can literally calm down physical reactions related to charged emotions and let your body *and* mind relax!

Here's an example: You're anxious about something. Maybe it's an important conversation you need to have, or you're feeling a stampede of butterflies in your belly as you prepare to speak or sing onstage for the first time.

Use your focused attention to scan your body. Look for areas that are "lit up" or stand out in some way. Often your stomach will be tight. You might also notice your heart pounding, your eye twitching, or your mouth feeling like someone dumped a bag of sand into it.

Start naming each sensation:

> "That's a Dry Mouth... There's Faster Heart Rate... Oh, the Whirlies...hello. Tight Stomach... The Niagara Falls of Sweat."

Again, you're *detaching* yourself from your physical symptoms by "calling them out," so to speak. The *present* moment returns. You remember to breathe... and maybe even smile.

The Third "D": *Detour*

> *"I got the blues thinking of the future, so I left off*
> *and made some marmalade. It's amazing how it*
> *cheers one up to shred oranges and scrub the*
> *floor."* – D. H. Lawrence

The 3rd "D" is *Detour*. This "D" is all about steering your attention *off* the Mind Loop Highway, and re-routing it toward something you *choose* to focus on.

This may sound simple, but it takes conscious effort. Because your mind isn't likely to let go of the loop so easily. You need to *detour* your attention while your Mind Loop is trying to lure you back.

Don't give in! *Detouring* is where you get to create that new Hiking Trail. It's KEY to rewiring your brain.

Dr. Daniel Amen agrees: "Whenever you find your thoughts cycling, (going over and over), distract yourself from them. Get up and do something else. Distraction is often a very helpful technique."[15]

To return to our hiking analogy, this is when you turn toward that new trail in the woods and actually start hiking it. It takes conscious effort at first because you'll be bushwhacking your way through, whereas the original trail (the Mind Loop) is well-worn, clear, comfortable, and easy to follow. But you *know* the new trail has more variety, bounty, and interest. More joy. Keep with it and you'll reach the ripest, most juicy huckleberries around.

What is your new route going to look like? What new thoughts and activities will you focus on instead of going back over the same old terrain in your Mind Loop? You have lots of choices. Create a *Detour List* of ideas that engage your mind, and support, empower, and inspire you so you'll be set up for success and less likely to fall back into the automatic pull of an old Mind Loop.

Why make an actual list? Because when a Mind Loop threatens your serenity, or triggers a distressing emotion, you're no longer in a healthy, creative space to brainstorm ideas. Creating the *Detour List* in advance, when you're in a clear frame of mind, means it will be there when you need it.

Here are a few examples to get you started:

Detour List Ideas

- Get busy on a project you love to do (art, music, cooking, genealogy, crafts...).
- Listen to upbeat music and dance around the house, exercise or spruce up your home.
- Move your body (work out, skip, dance, do yoga, stretching, play some hoops).
- Get outside (hike, bike, swim, garden, swing – or just walk around the block and notice the beauty around you).
- Feed your mind by taking in an inspiring talk (audiobook, TED, youTube, podcast), or movie, video

or book.

- Reach out to a friend, family member or acquaintance for a quick Detour conversation – ask about *their* day. (No bringing up your Mind Loop in that conversation. Remember, this is a Detour! If you need to, and it's appropriate, ask him/her to help you keep focused on other topics of conversation).

- If you're in a mood where nothing seems to inspire you, try starting a little project you've been meaning to do: Clean out a drawer, make a box of things to donate, call your (fill-in-the-blank), pull those weeds... You'll be surprised how often you end up getting into it. Before you know it, you're in a different frame of mind and you've gotten something off your list!

Make Your Own *Detour* List

Now it's your turn! As you make your own Detour List, you may want to check out the "Mega List of Detour Ideas" included in the Mind Loops Workbook to help you ignite your own ideas and passion:

http://www.MindLoopsWorkbook.com.

Once you've written your list, set yourself up for success by making sure all the supplies you'll need are accessible and ready to go. More detailed notes about this are also available in the Workbook.

The Foundation Is Laid

The first 3 "D's" work together like a finely-tuned instrument to uncover and then root out the loops that are puncturing holes in your happiness:

> *Detect* your negative thoughts, emotions, and loops;
>
> *Detach* from the loops with an Interruption Technique;
>
> *Detour* your thoughts immediately away from the loop to something that interests or inspires you – or even just gets you busy.

The more quickly you can catch yourself "in the act" of a Mind Loop, the easier it will be to stop them. That's key! It's like when you feel a cold coming on, and you know you can avert it or at least keep it from getting worse by loading up on vitamins, healthy food, sleep, and extra water.

The same is true with Mind Loops. The sooner you can recognize that a loop is starting up – and work the first 3 "D's" on it – the less power it'll have to hook you, grow its nasty roots into your consciousness, and lay you up for the next few days, if not months or years. You don't have to live like that anymore.

And *congratulate* yourself each time you catch yourself in a Mind Loop – even if it's tempting to say, "I wish I'd caught it earlier." You will, next time. For now, you're well on your way to getting free.

If the first 3 "D's" of De-Looping are like diving in for a

deep, spring cleaning on your house, the 4th "D" is like the Grand Remodel. And like most remodels, this "D" is going to take a little bit more time and explanation.

Our lives resemble works of great literature. Whether we realize it or not, we're the *authors* of much of what we experience – or more specifically, the authors of how we *interpret* our experiences.

With the 4th "D", *De-Story*, you become a *conscious* author of your life.

The Fourth "D": *De-Story*

> *"If you change the way you look at things, the*
> *things you look at change."*
> – Dr. Wayne Dyer

At one point in time, everyone believed the earth was flat. Terror struck the hearts of anyone who even *considered* sailing around the world because not only would they fall off the face of the earth via gigantic waterfalls, but the Atlantic Ocean was filled with horrific monsters large enough to devour their ships!

At one point everyone also believed the earth was the center of the universe... That women weren't "intelligent enough" to vote... Electricity was a figment of someone's far-out imagination...

These historical misconceptions might sound humorous to us now, <u>but they began as absolute beliefs, even *facts*</u>. So much so, that history is filled with people who were unfairly persecuted (like dear ol' Galileo) – facing imprisonment, torture and even death just for challenging the status quo.

Right or wrong, our personal and cultural beliefs often begin as *stories* that we hear or tell ourselves so often that those old "hiking trails" get paved with cement and turn into spiffy park walkways that don't allow even one little weed (or alternative viewpoint) to pop through.

Obviously, we all know differently now about the historical examples given above... Which *could* give us pause about our current beliefs and "facts," right? Are they all truly *true*?

The purpose of *De-Story* is to look more deeply into the stories you tell yourself to see which ones are holding you back, causing relationship or other problems, or triggering Mind Loops – and then *reframe* the story so you can finally let it go.

Stories Are Everywhere

> *"Whatever you perceive, you always make a
> story with yourself as the main character, and
> that dictates your life."* – Don Miguel Ruiz

All of us make up stories. We don't *call* them "stories", but that's really what they are. We call them memories, beliefs, social rules and conventions ("That's just the way things are *done*"). We string these things we "know" together in our minds until we create a specific worldview all our own, a cohesive story that makes sense and looks real and "right" to us.

The problem is, we forget that *alternate versions* may exist. And those alternate versions may support us a whole lot more than the versions we continually tell ourselves.

Once you start looking for "stories," you'll notice them *everywhere* – in your thoughts, in what you say to other people, and coming from the mouths of your friends, family, and coworkers.

Here are a few examples from my clients' lives:

Story: "She didn't text me back because she thinks I'm a idiot."

Reality: This client later received a text from the woman, apologizing for not texting: She had a house-guest who "borrowed" her phone without telling her. Meanwhile, this fellow looped on what an "idiot" he was and how he didn't deserve this woman for 24 hours – until he received her response.

Story: "I'm just not a very good musician."

Reality: This client earned a masters degree in music, graduated cum laude, plays 6 different instruments (strings, wind, brass, plus singing), and taught herself how to compose.

Story: "I'm too old to learn how to sing" (or start a business, start dating again, or any other dream you might have).

Reality: Pharrell Williams was a successful producer/songwriter for years, but didn't become a household name until he came out with his song, "Happy" at 40 years old; Colonel Sanders was 62 when he started Kentucky Fried Chicken; and Martha Stewart got onto Match.com at age 71.

You could write a whole book of all the people that have proved this story wrong. It's never too late to start something you're passionate about! Not to mention that this type of "I can't do something I love because..." story has the power to stop you in your tracks and lead to immense regret later on for things *not* done.

We Love Our Stories

I asked a new client the other day, "Are you *ready* to be happy?"

He paused. "I'd like to *believe* I'm ready..." But then his voice trailed off. After a big sigh, he realized he was unable to answer the question. After more discussion, it became clear to us both that his story of "I'm unhappy, depressed, and a loser" had become such a key part of his identity that he wasn't sure what life would be like – or ask of him – if he couldn't say that anymore. He wanted to move on from that reality, but because it had become a foundation for his life, it felt scary to let it go.

We've spent so many years growing attached to our "stories" that we don't consider whether they're helping or hindering us – or even whether they're our own story or someone else's that we've adopted as our own. They've become *part of our identity* – like a barnacle that's attached itself to us. So it can be hard to give them up.

In some strange way, they've become comfortable – even if

they're painful. They're "what we know."

"War Stories"

> *"I spent an unhappy, penniless childhood in*
> *Brooklyn. I had to slug my way up in a town*
> *called Hollywood where people love to trample*
> *you to death."* – Susan Hayward

One type of story people often tell and re-tell are "war stories." Not *actual* war stories, but past hardships – tough childhoods, nasty ex-lovers, or emergency situations we escaped from in the nick of time, like being mugged, or a teenager "joyride" that went bad.

There are some definite benefits to telling our "war stories" from time to time:

- By re-living them, we're reminding ourselves – and expressing to others – that we survived something big. And not just that we survived it – but *how* we survived it reveals so much about what kind of person we are. It's proof we have a tremendous amount of strength and resilience in us.

- When we share a "war story" with a person we trust, it can feel like a big weight has been lifted, because our secrets can eat us up inside. And it's a form of intimacy; we don't feel so alone.

- We can also gain insight into our own patterns and choices by delving into them (as in therapy).

- Finally, war stories are usually anything but normal. People's eyes widen when you tell them... They want more juicy details, they shake their heads in disbelief... War stories can be smokin' hot tales to tell!

These are all great reasons to bring up your war stories *from time to time*. The problem is, many of us don't just visit these stories every so often. We *dwell* on them. And that has a giant pitfall:

<u>Dwelling on your war stories can keep you stuck in Mind Loops</u>.

It's important to detach from these painful stories so you can focus *forward* on the life you're creating *now*: A life befitting the New You that's emerging as you release your Mind Loops.

De-Story Is NOT About Denying That Something Happened

This is an important point I want to make:

<u>De-Story is not about denying that something happened</u>.

I'm a huge proponent of *not* sweeping things under the rug. This also isn't about re-writing part of your history just because it's ugly. The whole idea behind *De-Story* is to look at

DE-LOOP WITH THE FIRST 4 STEPS

the stories you tell *over and over* – to yourself, your family, your partner, your friends – and decide if they're adding to, or subtracting from, your life.

So many times there's no *movement* with our stories. They're just the same old tale looping over and over – painfully. There may be specific *factual* occurrences in your life that were extremely difficult and can't be changed; what's done is done. It's your *interpretation* of these events and your *response* to them that we'll be examining and re-negotiating. If your story is locked in stone, if it's unmoving and unchanging – *and* it's also painful, stressful, self-limiting, and self-defeating – then *for your own happiness and wellbeing,* I say it could use a little *de-storying.*

The 4ᵗʰ "D" can be magical... and provide a lot of relief.

Six Big Reasons Why De-Story Is So Important

When you *de-story* your "stories"...

1) <u>your talents, ambitions, opportunities, and openness to love can suddenly expand and have a chance to thrive</u>. Because it's your story-*loops* that put you down, or bring up scary scenarios (past or present) that stop you from moving out of your comfort zone and toward what you desire.

2) <u>your confidence, happiness, serenity and courage can grow stronger</u>. Because they're no longer being

pushed down by the constant reinforcement of the old negative beliefs your life or character was based on.

3) you can connect more deeply with others because your ability to love, feel compassion, and engage with other people expands. Our "stories" can be judgment *machines*, and when we (unconsciously) pre-judge others or make assumptions about their intentions, it automatically limits our ability to connect with them. Forgiveness is an amazing feeling!

4) you automatically lower your stress! When we create stories, we're often misinterpreting situations in ways that disempower us – and that's stressful! Higher stress levels lead to: feeling exhausted, more wrinkles, lowered immune function (more allergies, coughs, colds & flu, or worse), restless sleep, and chronic grumpy face.

5) you can become more flexible with social "rules" – which leads to more ease in relationships. Many of your social rules are stories that were "installed" when you were too young to choose whether you even agreed with them. They can become dictators in your life as you become unreasonable with yourself and others, sometimes without even knowing it.

6) create those wonderful "Ah-ha!" moments, where it feels like a veil has been lifted from your view of reality. Stories disguise themselves as *reality* – we

believe there's only one interpretation of a situation, and it can't be changed. When you de-story, you find out the truth... It can.

When you de-story, you'll be looking at memories, beliefs, judgments, and social rules from new perspectives. You'll then have the choice to stay with that story you've been telling yourself (a fine and valid choice if that's what you really want)...

Or to *choose* a different story once you see other possibilities. Life is *all about* choices – and CHOICE is where your place of power lies.

How To De-Story

Since there are a lot of different "brands" of stories out there, we'll be covering four different ways you can use *De-Story* in your life, depending on which stories are holding you back the most. Each method will help tremendously to shift your perspective on past or present challenges. (Not everyone will have struggles in all four areas, so just see what fits for you and your life).

De-Story Method 1: A Diamond In the Making.

This section covers negative memories/stories you may be holding onto about how other people have wronged you. It could be a parent, an ex-lover, sibling, boss or colleague; anyone from a past or current situation who you're having trouble forgiving.

De-Story Method 2: **The Mystery of Memory.**

This part helps with painful memories, with a focus on childhood.

De-Story Method 3: **The Umwelt.**

If you often think to yourself, "That person isn't doing it right!" take a look at this section.

De-Story Method 4: **De-Story To De-Stress.**

This one is for you if you're feeling really stressed out and overwhelmed.

What Makes a Great Story?

First, let's look at what makes up a great story, so you can not only *change* your stories, but transform them into something *great*.

If you think about your favorite novels and films, what makes them so engaging and satisfying?

Sure, the drama is intriguing, the terror, conflict and heartbreak... But often it's a *thumbs-down* if the protagonist goes through their ordeal and in the end just *suffers* with it, re-living the pain every chance they get for the rest of their life.

Those kinds of "Happy Never After" stories leave you with an unsettled feeling that can be hard to shake. We always want to believe we can do better than just "get by" or just *survive* the more difficult circumstances in our lives.

Great stories – from "Star Wars" to "Pride and Prejudice" – follow the character through their hardship... and they don't just survive, but they *grow* because of it, and *come out better than before*. Possibly even make the world a better place because of their actions.

Maybe the character grew into a more compassionate, generous, loving person... Or all that heartbreak led them to meet the true love of their life... Or they fulfilled their destiny by conquering the 18-legged mutant monster-squid, saving the town from destruction, and becoming a great leader in the process.

Some *benefit* came from the hardship that made it worthwhile in the end.

If you're thinking: "Sure, that works in fiction. But what about *real* life? Some bad things happened to me. We can't change those memories... can we?"

Let's find out.

De-Story Methods

De-Story Method 1:
A Diamond In the Making

"I don't want to come across as a victim with a
sob story. I thank the bullies out there for
making me who I am. Some people become
weaker, but the bullies made me stronger."
– Kierston Wareing

D iamonds start out as lumps of rock buried under more than 100 miles of heavy earth. They endure temperatures of at least 2,000 degrees F. They refuse to shatter even under a weight of 54,000 times atmospheric pressure. And the only reason we find diamonds at all is because they're carried to the surface of the earth from a super-fast volcanic eruption that travels at twice the speed of sound!

It's the difficult and painful experiences of intense force, heat, speed and "trauma" that diamonds go through that transform them into the rare, glistening stones we cherish.

You're like that diamond. You survived the volcanic explosion – the dark years of that bad marriage, difficult childhood, demeaning jobs that didn't value who you were, the long illness, the bullies, that heartbreaking loss that nearly brought you to your knees.... You came through it all and you're still here. That's the first step. Congratulations! Seriously.

Your Greatest Teachers, Gifts, and Foes

"Our enemies are our greatest teachers."
- Dalai Lama

In his don Juan books, Carlos Castaneda often talked about our opponents (the people who challenge us the most, trip us up, anger us) appearing in our lives specifically to be our teachers.

If you had a difficult time with your parents or siblings or neighborhood bullies, just for a moment, *pretend* they were a teacher you hired (but of course your dog chewed up the contract and it was so long ago you forgot you'd ever hired them).

Ask yourself: "What did that person teach me about myself, about life? What did I learn about myself from the hardships I've endured? What skills did I learn *because* that person was in my life? How was my direction altered by their presence in my life?"

You may discover you learned a *lot*. And you may even be using what you learned to amazing benefit in your life without realizing it.

A Love Story

"You don't need to change the world; you need to change yourself." – Miguel Ruiz

Brandi, an intelligent, attractive woman, was drawn to charismatic men. It would always start out well, but within a year her self-esteem would crash as her partner started using his charms on other women, disregarding her.

When we started working together and looked at her "stories" about love, she revealed a terrible heartbreak as a teenager that still haunted her, even after all these years. It left her with this story:

"Why try this again? Men can't be trusted. Love always fails in the end."

As we began interrupting these damaging Mind Loops and shifting her story about love, her self-esteem blossomed. She finally started to see herself for the amazing woman she is. As a result, she was able to set clear boundaries and focus on her own joy rather than the fear of losing a relationship. Her inner "guy-picker" shifted too, and for the first time she found a man worthy of her fabulous self.

Brandi is happier and stronger now than she's ever been. She was able to not only forgive the men she felt had "done her wrong," but even feel gratitude to them for the role they played in revealing where she needed to grow and change in order to find real happiness.

If It's Easy, It's a Gift: Drums and the Funny Guy

"Adversity has the effect of eliciting talents –
which in prosperous circumstances would have
lain dormant." – Horace

Every one of us has certain skills and abilities that are so easy for us, they feel more like breathing than a skill. Rarely do we realize that those talents are often the result of coping with tough situations.

Your troubles may have led you to develop unique talents, driving you to study and practice with such a ferocity that you gained mastery in a skill you might never have tried if your life had been less "eventful."

Or your struggles may have turned into such a deep passion and understanding of the problem, that you now help others cope with the same type of trials you sweated out. (Case in point: My own battle with Mind Loops has enabled me to help others deal with theirs).

Wherever your pain led you often becomes your greatest gift – and sometimes your "life purpose."

"My music had roots which I'd dug up from my own childhood, musical roots buried in the darkest soil." – Ray Charles

Robert began playing drums when he was a very young kid. Perhaps that's not so uncommon... Except the *intensity* he had for it *was* uncommon:

Every day as soon as he'd get home from school, he'd start practicing his drums – often not getting up from the kit for *six hours straight*. One *story* to explain this wild passion is that he was unconsciously redirecting anger about a rough home life into a musical obsession.

Can you guess what happened? He became a stunningly talented and sought-after drummer.

Maybe Robert would have reached that level of mastery without the complications at home... But if things had been all hunky dory, he might have preferred riding his bike and digging for worms with his buddies rather than staying inside alone, diligently banging away on his drum set hour after hour, day after day.

History is filled with artists who turned (sometimes in desperation) to their creativity to help them deal with challenging circumstances. As a result, their talents were often defined, refined, and honed into something truly exceptional.

"Comedy comes from a place of hurt. Charlie Chaplin was starving and broke in London, and that's where he got his character 'the tramp' from. It's a bad situation that he transformed into a comedic one."

– Chris Tucker

Adam was the overweight, clumsy kid who was the butt of everyone's jokes in grade school. Bullies waited for him after class for weeks. It seemed like no matter what he did to turn the situation around – to be smart or "cool" in front of the other kids – it would backfire on him.

Until he started blurting out jokes.

They began as self-deprecating one-liners... And developed into a well-defined humor that would crack up the entire class. After years of heartache and isolation, Adam had found a unique gift that made even the popular kids slap him on the back as one of their own.

He went on to study filmmaking and eventually worked as a successful comedy sketch writer.

De-Story Your Opponents and Struggles: Discover the Gifts

"All battles in life serve to teach us something, even the battles we lose." – Paulo Coelho

Now it's your turn. Look at some tough situations you've dealt with. What did you learn about yourself by dealing with *your* life's opponents? If they were your "teachers," what was the "curriculum"? What strengths did you gain? How did working through those conflicts sharpen your ability to deal with people later on?

It helps to start by simply *accepting* what occurred. Yes, the experience happened. *But it's not happening to you right now.* To borrow (and slightly alter) a famous phrase from 12-step groups: "This too DID pass." It's over now. You're still here.

How you dealt with those hard knocks – and deal with them *now* – is *often is the key to unlocking your greatest gift(s)*.

If it's a current situation, what might this "opponent" be doing in your life right now? If that person was a messenger who came to reveal something to you, what might that message be?

Instead of letting the situation continue to rob you of your power and life energy, how might you turn it around so it becomes a source of *empowerment* for you?

See De-Story Exercise #1: "Uncover Your Hidden Gifts" in the Mind Loops Workbook for more on uncovering skills and gifts you gained from a difficult childhood. It'll help you view those experiences in a very different light.

Also see De-Story Exercise #2: "A Worthy Opponent" in the Workbook for help with recent (adulthood) experiences that are causing headaches or worse in your life.

De-Story Method 2:
The Mystery of Memory

"Memory is not pure. Memories told are not pure memories; memories told are stories. The storyteller will change them."
– Alice McDermott

"Human memory is a marvelous but fallacious instrument. The memories which lie within us are not carved in stone; not only do they tend to become erased as the years go by, but often they change, or even increase by incorporating extraneous features." – Primo Levi (scientist)

There's a ton of fascinating research on how memories are created and stored, as well as how they *change*. Yes, memories can and do change over time. They're *malleable*.

We have this belief that memories are like files you pull out and they're always the same. The reality is, every time you think or talk about a memory, you're *re-writing* it a little bit.

When you put that memory back into "storage," the memory isn't quite the same. You won't *know* you've shifted it, but in some subtle way, you have.

It's like that old "Telephone" game you played in kindergarten, where one kid whispers a sentence in the ear of the next kid, who passes on what s/he hears into the next kid's ear. By the time the last kid receives the message and says the sentence out loud, everyone bursts into laughter because the original sentence has turned into a different beast altogether!

It's also why you can reminisce with a sibling about a memory from childhood and have this strange interaction:

"Remember when Mom bought us those ice cream cones and you dropped all 3 scoops on the ground and burst out crying?" And your sibling will say, "That wasn't *me*! That was *you* who dropped the ice cream and started crying!"

And then you look at each other like the other person is bonkers.

Not only do we rewrite our memories all the time, but our brains unconsciously *"fill in"* details that *weren't actually remembered but still feel like fact*.[16]

I realize that's a strange idea to ponder. But here's how it can benefit you:

Memories don't have to be (and *aren't*) "written in stone." It's more like they're made of soft clay – and you get to be the sculptor, depending on *what you choose to focus on*.

Changing Memories *Consciously*

> *"I've come to believe that if you have a bad*
> *memory of something, change it."*
> – Liza Minnelli

We can look at memories from any angle we want. Maybe you've been looping on a bad memory *as viewed through a distorted, cloudy window for years.* And every time you re-live that memory, your body feels a rush of adrenaline, your heart starts pounding, and emotions like humiliation, shame, or anger pop up – even though the experience happened 30 years ago.

And every time you replay these negative memories (stories), you're strengthening the first "hiking trail" in your brain; you're solidifying that neural pathway... And that means you're creating a *long-term* memory.

But when you look at the same memory through a *different* window – one with a broader view – you might see something altogether different; something less villainous.

And each time you "re-store" the memory, it'll be a shade different than when you pulled it out last.

Keep doing this, and slowly the memory will literally *change.*

There was a time when I would loop about painful events that occurred during my childhood. Re-living those memories again and again would make me feel angry, depressed, and resentful. And then I started to *de-story* those memories...

I'm astonished to say that it now takes concerted *effort* to pull up any negative memories from my early years. I see so much humor in it all now! I've forgiven the characters in my story and feel greater compassion for all of us. I recognize how much I learned from it, what gifts my family gave me, and how much I grew from my experiences. I now view the whole scenario with deep love and appreciation. As a result, the love I already felt for my family has expanded and deepened.

Once you've "mined" your old memories for their lessons and gifts, are there some left over that you're eager to "rewrite"? Let's begin by finding a more interesting and satisfying window to view them from.

De-Story Your Childhood Memories: 9,460,800 Minutes

> *"Childhood is a tricky business. Usually,*
> *something goes wrong."*
> – Maurice Sendak

For some of us, when we think about our childhoods, they can feel like one long, 18-year train wreck. Memories are filled with negativity, trauma and hurtful comments and behaviors that we had to endure.

But guess what? You experienced 9-million, 460-thousand, 800 minutes in your first 18 years of life. Is it possible there were, say, *90 minutes* in there that were actually fun?

Creative? Triggered some cool fascination or curiosity in you? Maybe you even felt... happy?

Every time we think about all the crappy things that happened, they crowd out the good memories – sometimes to oblivion. To re-balance and empower yourself regarding your whole childhood "package," sort through those 9-million-plus minutes and find some moments that were actually *good*.

Write them down. Really *ponder* them. Dwell on them to the same degree you dwell on the negative aspects of childhood. Get all of your senses involved. Look for details in the memory. Let those wonderful moments fill your heart. They may lead you to other delightful childhood memories you had forgotten.

This takes conscious effort. But it's well worth it. Because when you de-story your childhood, it reconfigures your present.

And by the way, this technique works for *any* period of time that contains painful memories: It can be childhood or adulthood, from years ago, or something that happened just last week.

See De-Story Exercise #3: "Find 10" in the Workbook for more in-depth help on stopping loops on bad memories.

De-Story Method 3:

The Umwelt

There's a fabulous German word: *Umwelt*. While it means "environment" in German, it refers to our assumption that our own personal reality is the only true reality out there.

So often as we go through life, we think we're *right*. We think we know the whole story, when in fact we're filling in gaps left and right with assumptions about other people's motives, feelings, thoughts, and behaviors – based on *our own filters, experiences, and belief systems.*

Even when our "stories" are based on what the other person *tells* us about themselves, how could we possibly understand the *whole* story – even if we've been through something similar? We can't. Because we're still interpreting their words and experiences through *our own view of the world.*

It's hard enough to understand everything there is to know about *ourselves* – let alone another person! We're just too complex, too multi-layered, and grow up with such varied thoughts, emotions, experiences and beliefs, that to think we could truly grasp another person's *umwelt* is unrealistic. And yet we do it all the time. "Storytelling" is in our blood!

And that can create big problems – and big Mind Loops.

The "He's Too Cool For School" Guy... And the "Happiest Couple In the World!"

> *"Truth is, I'll never know all there is to know*
> *about you, just as you will never know all there*
> *is to know about me. Humans are by nature too*
> *complicated to be understood fully. So, we can*
> *choose either to approach our fellow human*
> *beings with suspicion or to approach them with*
> *an open mind, a dash of optimism and a great*
> *deal of candor."*
> – Tom Hanks

Have you ever met someone who seemed just "too cool for school"? That guy who's *oh-so-cool* and disinterested in everything to the point that he's arrogant and rude and every time you see him, he blows you off? A-hole!

So of course you tell everyone about what a jerk he is, how he's so full of himself, and won't smile at you or anyone else *because he thinks he's so above everyone.*

Then one day, you actually *meet* this person and you get a real chance to talk. It's then you discover just how wrong your assumptions were. To your surprise, you find he's actually an amazing person. Not only that, but he reveals to you just how shy and awkward and even *anxious* he feels in social settings.

Guess he wasn't "too cool for school" after all. Just shy.

If something like this has happened to you, you know how your story about that person changes – and in an instant. Now your story about that person is one of compassion instead of disdain.

And if *you* were the one who was misunderstood, maybe you can understand a little better how these things can happen. It doesn't mean "the world is against you." Just that we're all still growing and learning, all the time.

Then there's the "Happiest Couple In the World" story.

Here, you have two friends who seem to be the "perfect couple." Every time you see them, there's so much laughter and closeness, you walk away thinking, "Wow, they're so incredible together... What an extraordinary love!"(And maybe, "If only I could find that for myself... Life is so unfair!")

Next thing you know, you get an email: "Brandon and I are splitting up. It's been a long time coming, and we finally decided it's best for both of us."

What?! *The happiest couple in the world?!*

So often we look at someone else's life from the outside and we think we know what's going on. But we don't.

That goes for their *inner* lives as well: We can never know what thoughts they're actually thinking, nor what deep despair, anger, heartache, fear, or low self-esteem they may be feeling.

Even the most successful, joyful people have fears and bad days. It's called being human.

De-Story Your Memories and Assumptions About Other People

"You never really understand a person until you consider things from his point of view... Until you climb inside of his skin and walk around in it." – Harper Lee

What would happen if you stepped into the shoes of another person, even for a moment?

The next time you have a "situation" to deal with, use the power of your imagination to slip into the other person's *umwelt* and try to view the world from their point of view.

How does this change your story about the situation? Are you now open to at least other *possible* explanations for that person's behavior?

This technique also works for past memories. If you loop on situations from your past that still have the power to get you all worked up, try stepping into that other person's shoes. What do you suppose they were really thinking or feeling at the time? How does this change your story?

See De-Story Exercise #4: "Change Your Shoes" in the Workbook to shift negative thoughts and feelings about relationships, interactions, and memories.

De-Story Method 4:

De-Story To De-Stress

"Remember that stress doesn't come from your boss, your kids, your spouse, traffic jams, health challenges, or other circumstances. It comes from your <u>thoughts</u> about these circumstances."
– Andrew J. Bernstein

S tress is a natural part of our existence as humans. But *chronic* stress is a whole other animal. And Mind Loop "stories" are a potent culprit in creating chronic stress.

When you're "stressed out," what's actually happening is your fight-or-flight response has gotten triggered. That means your sweet body gets a *surge* of adrenaline, cortisol, and other "stress hormones" that can make you feel miserable physically, emotionally, and mentally.

Obnoxious effects of chronic stress range from:

- snapping at others like an angry turtle

- wanting nothing more than to stay in bed with the covers over your head for days on end
- headaches that feel like wrecking balls slamming against your temples
- waking up every night at 2am to ponder the wretchedness of life
- high blood pressure (a Big Nasty that can lead to heart attacks or stroke)
- zero interest in your favorite foods
- zero interest in moving your body (physical exercise, dancing, sports, sex)
- tight muscles that feel more like cement blocks lodged under your skin
- overdoing it and trying to "fix" the way you feel with food, drugs, alcohol, shopping, et al
- and more colds and flus than a grade school teacher.

Yippee! Can't wait to join *that* party!

It's Not Just the Big Events

We all know stress comes with the Big D's: Divorce, death, and disease. But it also comes from events that we just *perceive* as stressful. That means Mind Loops.

Like when you re-live a bummer memory, or keep stewing about an upcoming event.

You can trigger a stress (and Mind Loop) response just by

fretting over what others might say about you after you post your new video on YouTube, or give that presentation at work – even whether that purple polka dot tie and red pants are too much for the occasion.

When we engage in "stories," it's like fanning a stress flame in our bodies and minds. We're repeating the negative thoughts so much that our nervous system doesn't have a chance to return to normal. It believes we're constantly in a life-threatening circumstance. Voila! Chronic stress.

It's All Relative

Have you ever had a day like this?

You sleep through your alarm, spill coffee on yourself while getting into your car, and forget there's an important morning meeting, so now you walk into it late...

...Then you find that your co-workers haven't finished the project you needed so instead of the accolades you hoped for from your boss you get The Look and a humiliating finger-wag...

...At lunch, the jerk in front of you takes the last serving of your favorite dish...

...And finally as you're on your commute home, you get stuck in freeway traffic because of some damn accident in the rain! "Arrgh! I hate my job... life... the world!"

Until... The traffic creeps up to where the police and ambulance lights are flashing... Right then, you see a young woman being taken out of the smashed car on a stretcher.

Suddenly you imagine all the dreams and projects that woman was passionately in the middle of that will now be put on hold – if she makes it at all. You think of her loved ones, and how this nightmarish accident will affect them.

In an instant, all the irritants that happened to you today seem so petty and ridiculous.

De-Story Your Stress: What a Great Problem To Have!

Putting your situation in perspective is one of the *speediest* ways to get yourself out of a Mind Loop. There's probably always someone dealing with something far worse than what you're dealing with right now.

See De-Story Exercises #5: "What a Great Problem To Have!" in the Workbook for a more in-depth explanation of how to work with *relativity* to shift your perspective and lower your stress.

Unnecessary Stress:
The Case of the Missing Thank-You Cards and Green Napkins

"It is almost as important to know what is not serious as to know what is."

- John Kenneth Galbraith

I have a friend who sadly was dealing with breast cancer at one time. She had just undergone a mastectomy. Friends and family sent cards, flowers and gifts to cheer her up. When I arrived to visit her, she was stressed out. I thought it was about the cancer. That was obviously a lot of it – but she was also deeply upset with the fact that she had so many thank you cards to write and no energy to do it!

"What?!" I responded incredulously. "No one's expecting you to write them thank you cards! All their gifts were to help you feel better – not to stress you out even more!"

One of my clients would also feel like she let people down if her social graces weren't "perfect." She loved giving dinner parties, but would invariably feel high levels of anxiety beforehand. She told me how one evening she realized she had only seven matching green napkins for a sit-down dinner – and 10 guests were coming. That little detail threw her into a terrible Mind Loop tailspin – so much so that her husband suggested she contact me after the party.

Whether or not you can relate to these examples, there's a lot of emotion underlying them. The pain of wanting to be "perfect," "right," or just accepted by others can get even the best of us.

De-Story Your Stress: We Make the Unimportant, Important

Social rules can run amuck and cause completely unnecessary

arguments, resentments, and stress. And they aren't the only area where we can get stuck not seeing the forest for the trees.

Are there areas in your life where you're making unimportant things, important?

See De-Story Exercise #6: "Ron's Message: Un/Important" in the Workbook for help getting clear on what's truly important – and when it's okay to bend the "rules" to gain more serenity.

******

De-Story Bottom Line

The bottom line for De-Story is asking these two simple questions:

- "Does the story I'm telling myself (and everyone else) serve me?"

If not...

- "Is it at least *possible* there's another version of this story that could serve me better?"

Often it's just as likely that another, more positive version of the situation is true. Humans tend toward the negative because of evolutionary reasons: It was more important to our survival to think about what could go wrong (a saber tooth tiger might be around that corner!) than about what could go right (these berries might taste really good!).

If it turns out that a different story *could* be true, and if it serves you better than the negative one you're telling yourself... Adopt it.

Give people the benefit of the doubt: Maybe they aren't purposefully trying to hurt you any more than you're trying to hurt others. Maybe they're stressed out and looping, or just plain unaware.

"Giving people the benefit of the doubt" includes you, too, by the way. What if you've been wrong about yourself – with your negative self-criticisms – all along? I challenge you to just *consider* the idea that your limiting ideas about yourself might not be true; that you really are a good person. *Fabulous,* in fact. And that you deserve a full, successful, happy life if for no other reason than *simply because you won the cosmic lottery and were given the gift of life.*

If *that* was your story about yourself, how might your behavior and outlook change?

De-Story is an incredible tool to use on a *daily basis.* Were you upset, felt disrespected, or blamed someone else for your own experience today? Use the De-Story tools to unravel your "umwelt" and view the situation through a different window.

Our stories reflect our choices. And they can flavor our days sweetly or sourly. Choose wisely.

PART FIVE:

Tips For De-Looping Success

W hat's the best way to get started with all of this info?

First: Download the free Mind Loops Workbook I created as a companion to this book at http://www.MindLoops Workbook.com. It's packed with practical tips, questions, and exercises that will help you:

- get more clarity about what to de-loop first
- support and expand your *de-storying* skills
- give you a method to chart your progress
- stay motivated and on-track with your de-looping program.

Next: Start with the first "D" (*Detect*) – but remember you don't have to make a complete inventory of all your negative thoughts right off the bat. Just begin the process of developing an awareness of your own loops.

3 Tips To Jumpstart Your De-Looping

Tip #1: First Things First

<u>What ONE area is causing you the most headaches and heartaches in your life?</u> Rollercoaster relationships? Skittish to accept invites to social events? Over-worrying about a specific issue? Start there.

Start tuning into the thoughts that gun their engines whenever that ONE issue rears its ugly head – especially when you notice your emotions taking a nosedive.

Choose one of the Interruption Techniques (from the section on the 2nd "D", *Detaching*) to try out. Then <u>make an intention</u> to *Detach & Detour* from any negative thought related to that issue, whenever you catch it. Put up little post-its around the house or alerts on your phone to help remind yourself to *Detach*.

Use the exercises in the Workbook to uncover the "stories" you're telling yourself that are exacerbating this issue – and start *de-storying* them.

<u>If you begin with the first 4 "D's" on *one* challenge, you'll probably start shifting things pretty quickly</u>. Once there's more flow going on in that one area, you can start focusing on another area.

Tip #2: Track Your Progress

<u>Get a de-looping notebook</u> and start recording <u>specific Mind Loop phrases</u> you notice repeating in your head. Also record

your <u>progress</u> in the area you're de-looping, and the <u>insights</u> that arise.

Very important: Also write down the surprise strokes of luck that often start to occur, such as:

- The "perfect" person suddenly showing up in your life who helps create forward momentum in your business/career, love/relationship, a health issue or any other question that's stumping you;
- Opportunities, invitations, trips, gifts, found objects, etc, that appear out of nowhere;
- Long-held resentments finally disappearing with ease (after holding onto them for so long they're probably growing Mind Loop mold);
- Any and all successes – especially the ones related to the area in your life you're de-looping;
- Increased positive attention, including from strangers – like smiles, compliments, and any random act of kindness.

All of this will be important to look back on as you "detox" your negative thoughts and loops. Otherwise it's easy to forget what your starting line looked like, and just how far you've come.

Tip #3: **The Buddy System**

If possible, <u>find at least one other person</u> you can trust to help support you as you go through this program. Even better: Is there someone who might want to de-loop their own thoughts along with you? If so, it's like having a "gym buddy." (Except instead of developing great "guns," you'll each be developing a healthy new mind and happy heart).

A De-Looping Buddy System can be as simple as texting each other every day with little reminders ("Are you spying on your thoughts?" "Are you playing the Name Game? I just named my loop 'Stink Bomb!'").

You could also help each other *De-Story* your "war stories" and assumptions about other people by brainstorming ideas together of alternative reasons why someone may have acted a certain way.

And you could decide to be "Diversion Partners" together. This is when you make a pact to help divert the focus of the person who's looping with a lunch, movie, or other activity. If you make sure it's really mutual, it can be *very* effective. (More detail about this can be found in the full list of *Detour* suggestions in the Workbook).

CONCLUSION

"Action is the foundational key to all success."
– Pablo Picasso

Y ou just learned the first 4 "D's of De-Looping." After you work with them for a while, you may notice that you feel changed in ways that are clear and obvious to both you and others. There may be a sense that things will never be the same again – you've "seen the light," as they say, and you're never going back to Mind Loop hell.

Others will notice a more *subtle* shift. If your transformation is more gradual, with less obvious outer changes occurring, it may not seem like much is happening. You may even be questioning if anything's happening at all – especially if the same problems continue to pop up in your life.

Just keep working the 4 D's of De-Looping. It takes time to undo the neural pathways we've turned into 4-lane highways in our brains. Remember, you're creating brand new neural pathways after a lifetime of going down a different path. This doesn't happen overnight.

Be patient: When you develop the skill of taking back

control of your thoughts, you don't just stop looping, you get your life back.

You Don't Need To Do This Program *Perfectly* To Get the Benefits!

Even with all my talk about staying committed and consistent with these 4 "D"s, don't beat yourself up if you backslide! You don't have to do it *perfectly*. In fact, you won't. I *still* don't do it perfectly. So what? Just let that fantasy go. Humans always tend to learn as much or more from their "mistakes" as they do from their successes. And as long as you're making progress in the right direction, that's all that matters.

As Harry Truman said, "Imperfect *action* trumps perfect *inaction*." Just notice you "fell off the horse," and get back on again. *You haven't failed.* You're just being human.

Something you'll want to note, however, is what thoughts are going through your head if you start thinking about giving up the program. Remember "Godzilla" from earlier in the book – the part of your brain that loves to trip you up so it can stick with the old negative program? If you backslide a bit or are tempted to stop the program altogether, it's very possible your inner Godzilla may have come out of its cave and started to growl: "This is hard. It probably doesn't work anyway. Just give it up."

Don't try to push that voice away. You now know that trying to push away negative thoughts doesn't work! Instead, thank

Godzilla for its input, then *Interrupt* that inner voice, using the 4 "D's."

I've learned we need to *deeply* want to feel better in order to be motivated enough to do the difficult work of modifying our habits. Changing your old thought patterns isn't easy.

But when you start feeling happier, less overwhelmed, and have more energy and delight in life, the motivation to keep working this program will come much more easily.

And the more you choose to do what it takes to feel happier, your body, mind, and spirit will receive the message that *you're worth it.*

Life Is Like A Wave

Life goes up, life goes down. Some days you'll feel energized and confident and happy... Other days you'll feel unmotivated and low.

This is the way of life: Of breathing in and out, of waves rising and falling, of the sun going up, going down, and clouds that roll in and roll out.

It's no use getting bent out of shape when the "high" days slow down for a time. They simply will. The good news is that you know the "low" days will pass too.

Just keep this in mind when you wish life was different. It *will* change. It always does.

The point of this book is to give you the tools to keep your "low points" brief – and to not dip so low when they do come.

Mind Loops that in the past would have laid you up for days or weeks become *one* day, or *one* hour, or even just a brief blip in your life.

You have *great* power: The power of your conscious mind. Once you know how to redirect your thoughts, your life will change in ways you never expected. It has a domino effect. Because when your thoughts no longer stop you from doing what you love and yearn for, you begin to step out of the ever-encroaching comfort zone. Courage develops. Confidence. Self-esteem rises. You take more steps toward your goals and dreams, you experience successes. And when things don't go quite as planned, you recover much more quickly.

Most importantly, the challenges, mishaps, and bumps in the road will *no longer cause you to stop.* You'll no longer hold yourself back, or retreat from your desired goal. You'll gain strength.

It all begins with these first 4 "D's."

You can do this! You owe it to yourself, and to the dream of living your best life.

To Sum Up the Key Points In This Book:

The 1st "D": *Detect*

Technique: Spy On Your Thoughts

The 2nd "D": *Detach*

Interruption Technique: "My Left Foot"

Interruption Technique: "The Name Game"

The 3rd "D": *Detour*

Make a "Detour List"

The 4th "D": *De-Story*

De-Story Method 1: A Diamond In the Making

    De-Story Your "Opponents" and Struggles: Discover the Gifts

De-Story Method 2: The Mystery of Memory

    De-Story Your Childhood Memories

De-Story Method 3: The Umwelt

    De-Story Your Memories and Assumptions About Other People

De-Story Method 4: De-Story To De-Stress

    De-Story Your Stress: What a Great Problem To Have!

    De-Story Your Stress: We Make the Unimportant, Important

Next Steps

Clearing out your Mind Loops leaves space in your mind for "new and improved" thoughts and beliefs to enter that better reflect who you are today – and where you want to go.

So now is the time to start flooding your consciousness with thoughts that are more in line with the person you *want* to be and are moving towards being – whether that's happier, more confident, peaceful, playful, kind, adventurous...

How to do this? Consciously seek out and take in:

- Inspiring articles, videos, books, programs, etc.
- People who make you feel good. Watch out for anyone who brings your energy or mood down. Be aware of who you're surrounding yourself with, and which people pull you back into unwanted thinking habits.
- Figure out which activities bring your mood and energy *up,* and which activities bring you *down.* If you're addicted to TV and yet tend to feel sluggish or depressed afterwards, watch one hour less every day for a week. Do something else during that one hour – a bike ride, or read a novel that you've been told is a page-turner, or play an instrument – and observe how your mood and energy feel at the end of that week. Experiment with different activities. See what feels good.

The point is to *feed* your mind and heart! Find those things that bring you joy, and make it a priority to actually *do* them! Don't put off your happiness any longer. Yesterday is gone. Today is new. *Grab* today, cherish it. *Choose* to take these techniques and run with them.

You are the ruler of one thing: Your own mind. If you don't like the guest who has dropped by (fear, worry, doubt, insecurity), don't let them wander in even for a brief visit, because they might decide to move in for an extended stay. While you may not have a choice in what thoughts *come* to your mind's door, you do have the choice and *power* to shut the door on any uninvited guest right away – and invite in who you *want*.

And finally say this to yourself – like you mean it, out loud if possible – any time you need an extra boost:

"Yesterday is the LAST DAY I am going to suffer with these Mind Loops. Today is a NEW DAY, and now I choose differently. Life may throw me challenges – but I KNOW I can deal with them. I know how to Detect, Detach, Detour, and De-Story my thoughts. I know what to do.

I will FEED my mind! I will FEED my heart! I am strong, amazing, worthy. I develop more confidence, peace, and happiness, day by day. I know more good is coming my way. My luck is changing. My life is changing. I thank myself for being who I am. I'm so very thankful for being who I am, <u>exactly the way I am</u>, on this NEW day."

Final Thoughts...

"It's the game of life. Do I win or do I lose? One day they're gonna shut the game down. I gotta have as much fun and go around the board as many times as I can before it's my turn to leave." – Tupac Shakur

"No one can confidently say that he will still be living tomorrow." – Euripides

I want to leave you with the two most important awarenesses my near-death-experience brought home to me in its uniquely dramatic way:

Life is *unpredictable...* and *every moment* is precious.

When I chose to "come back" into my body and life, I thought: "Wow, I wasted so much time and energy on my Mind Loops before! I never want to waste even another *moment* on over-worrying, resenting, or letting my fear stop me ever again. And where did I ever get the notion that I could put off my dreams until I'm ready? What does "ready" even *mean*? (Is anyone *ever* ready?). What I want now is to *create as many spectacular memories as possible.*"

How about you?

No one has a crystal ball broadcasting how many days they have left to live. Do you really want to waste *another precious minute* criticizing yourself? Worrying what others think about you? Replaying painful moments from your past?

Do you really want to continue holding yourself back from the success you could be reveling in... Or the wild and fanciful surprises that life loves to serve up when we're open to them?

Wouldn't it be more fun to spend your time and energy creating as many spectacular memories as possible?

The wonderful speaker, Les Brown, said this powerful quote:

> *"The graveyard is the richest place on earth, because it is here that you will find all the hopes and dreams that were never fulfilled, the books that were never written, the songs that were never sung, the inventions that were never shared, the cures that were never discovered, all because someone was too afraid to take that first step, keep with the problem, or determined to carry out their dream."*

It can be scary to go for our dreams. It can feel *uncomfortable* to step out of our *comfort* zones – to do things differently, to *think* differently, to put yourself out there. But you don't have to *leap*. It just takes one step, one day, one choice, one "D" at a time.

Will you take that next step?

The fact you chose to get this book, at exactly this point in your life is an indicator that it's Your Time.

The world *needs* people who are willing to move forward in their lives and *go for it*. Because as you experience a full and rich life that's continually expanding in beauty and vitality, your happiness will light up not only you... But will also light up the path for others.

You deserve it, my friend.

Wishing you extraordinary success, peace... and happiness!

Barbara Ireland

AFTERWORD

Your Two Free Bonuses

To help you get the most out of the information in this book, I created a **Mind Loops Workbook** for you for FREE. It has exercises to help keep you on track and use the 4 "D's of De-Looping" most effectively. Download the Workbook if you're really serious about applying the 4 "D's of De-Looping" in your life: http://www.MindLoopsWorkbook.com.

I also created a second FREE bonus for you: A 20-minute, mp3 audiobook of Dr. Emmet Fox's inspiring text from 1935, **"The Seven-Day Mental Diet: How To Change Your Life In a Week."** (Yes, you got that right: "a *week*").

I chose this work because he beautifully clarifies how *all aspects of your life* change for the better once you start transforming your negative thoughts. It's a short listen, and very motivational – the perfect way to begin your Mind Loops Program. And hey, it's read by Yours Truly! Get it at: http://www.7daymentaldietbook.com.

Finally, join the conversation on the **Mind Loops**

Facebook Page! Share your experiences and breakthroughs, and ask for support when you need it. I'll be on there to answer questions too – we're all there to help and encourage you! http://www.Facebook.com/MindLoopsMentor.

The sooner you begin – while this book is still fresh in your mind – the sooner you'll start reaping the benefits of the 4 "D's".

Get started now. Happiness awaits you!

Want To Take De-Looping Further?

My own personal transformation has been the result of working diligently with these first 4 "D's" *in addition to* the other 5 steps in the "9 D's of De-Looping" system.

This book covers the first 4 "D's of De-Looping" because they're the foundational base to getting you feeling better *quickly*. On their own, they can shift a *lot*. Combine them with the other 5 "D's," and you'll have all the tools necessary to move toward your most cherished dreams and happiness. Here's a taste:

The next 2 "D's" of this 9-step program are about dissolving painful emotions from past events that are stuck in your body. You'll know you have these if you get emotionally "triggered" by a comment or situation and react more strongly than what the situation calls for – or if you continue to ruminate on past hurts, shame, or guilt.

The final 3 "D's" are the Reprogramming stage. This is

where you use the power of your brain's frontal lobe to gain clarity about what you want in life and who you want to be – and then start taking action toward creating the life you truly desire.

"D's" 5-9 are available in online courses and one-on-one mentoring. For more information on any of the Mind Loop programs, visit:

http://www.HowToStopNegativeThoughts.com.

Also, if you'd like inspiring and practical tips on living a Mind-Loop-free existence sent to your email, sign up for my bi-monthly articles by visiting:

www.HowToStopNegativeThoughts.com/blog.

******

FROM MIND LOOPS CLIENTS AND CLASS PARTICIPANTS:

"I finally feel at peace again! That feels like a miracle because I've been fighting for so long with these inexplicable emotions that don't even seem like who I am. I'm shocked at how messed up my mind got. Shocked. But I stopped looping! I'm so enjoying the relaxation!"
— Brett I, Seattle, WA

"I feel calmer. A lot less negative. Overall, I feel like I'm in a much more positive place than I have been in years. And I know that I will never be in a bad relationship again!! I can't thank you enough for putting yourself out there to do this!" —
Val C, Seattle, WA

"I felt lighter, even in the midst of a painful memory. I appreciate what you're offering us!"
— Karen J, Seattle, WA

"You embody what you espouse, Barbara. You're present, your eyes are bright and your face is open. You're living proof that this works. It's invaluable to me — just what the doctor ordered." — Caleb S, Seattle, WA

"To all of you who, like myself, have certain self-defeating character traits, self-doubt, and self esteem issues that were handed down generation after generation... And yet you're someone who has dreams, and somewhere deep within yourself you believe you can realize them... Barbara's Mind Loops work will shut up those naysayer inner voices within you. It will set you free from your weaknesses and instead allow them to become pillars of your growth and future success. I've taken several classes of self help, and these Mind Loop tools are what are sending me over the last hurdle into living the life I knew I was here to live – instead of living in reaction to my environment. Take a leap! This is the place to find your way and learn great tools to help you enjoy your voyage through life!"

– Kevin Jewell, Paris France

"I feel uplifted, like anything is possible!"
– Michelle H, Seattle, WA

NOTES

1   "Autodidactic Hall of Fame," Autodidactic Press (2015); http://www.autodidactic.com/profiles/profiles.htm#Ei nstein

2   "Over the past two decades, the use of antidepressants has skyrocketed. One in 10 Americans now takes an antidepressant medication; among women in their 40s and 50s, the figure is one in four." - Roni Caryn Rabin, "A Glut of Antidepressants," New York Times (8/12/2013); http://well.blogs.nytimes.com/2013/08/12/a-glut-of-antidepressants/

3   "A new report tracking antidepressant use among Americans from 2005-2008 found that more than 1 in 10 Americans ages 12 and older report taking an antidepressant medication. (Center for Disease Control and Prevention's (CDC's) National Health and Nutrition Examination Survey (NHANES))."

"As these new CDC data show, 11% of Americans aged 12 and older (3.7% of youth between 12 and 17) report taking antidepressants. Last year, antidepressants were the second most commonly prescribed medications, right after drugs to lower cholesterol." - Thomas Insel, "Director's Blog: Antidepressants: A complicated picture" (2011);

http://www.nimh.nih.gov/about/director/2011/antidep ressants-a-complicated-picture.shtml

4   "Globally, an estimated 350 million people of all ages suffer from depression." - WHO (World Health Organization) Fact sheet (2016); http://www.who.int/mediacentre/factsheets/fs369/en/

5   Dr. Joe Dispenza, You Are the Placebo: Making Your Mind Matter (Carlsbad: Hay House, 2014), 51.

6   Dispenza, You Are the Placebo, 51.

7   Dispenza, You Are the Placebo, 45.

8   Dispenza, You Are the Placebo, 99.

9   Dr. Bruce H. Lipton, The Biology of Belief: Understanding the Power of Consciousness, Matter & Miracles (Carlsbad: Hay House, 2008), 121

10 http://drjoedispenza.com/index.php?page_id=Evolve-Your-Brain

11 Takano & Tanno (2011). "Diurnal variation in rumination." Emotion Vol 11(5): 1046-1058; http://psycnet.apa.org/journals/emo/11/5/1046/

12 Dr. Daniel G. Amen, Change Your Brain Change Your Life: The Breakthrough Program for Conquering Anxiety, Depression, Obsessiveness, Anger, and Impulsiveness (New York: Three Rivers Press), 172.

13 http://www.mindful.org/jon-kabat-zinn-defining-

mindfulness/

14   Lieberman et al. 2007. "Putting Feelings Into Words:
     Affect Labeling Disrupts Amygdala Activity in Response
     to Affective Stimuli." UCLA;
     http://www.scn.ucla.edu/pdf/AL(2007).pdf

15   Amen, Change Your Brain Change Your Life, 172.

16   Taylor & Francis, "Your childhood memories are
     probably less accurate than you think." Science Daily
     (2014);
     http://www.sciencedaily.com/releases/2014/01/140127
     093027.htm

CREDITS AND ACKNOWLEDGMENTS

First, I want to thank my editor and extraordinary friend, Michele Padgette. Your insightful editing left me in awe and improved this book beyond measure. Not only that, but you have generously provided encouragement and support through all phases of my life – including my most difficult and "loopy" ones. Top it off with hundreds of hours of the deepest and most fantastical conversations any two people could ever have...! Your friendship is something I have "never read in a book, nor seen in a movie, nor..."

Dr. Joe Dispenza and Dr. Bruce Lipton: Your research and books have inspired me tremendously. My own de-looping really started to kick in once I read your material and finally began to understand the workings of my own brain and cells in a new way. The countless "Ah-ha!" moments I had while reading about your explorations into the human mind, body, and emotions, played a big part in the development of my "9 D's of De-Looping" system.

Thanks also to Drs. Daniel Amen and Alejandro Junger for their cutting-edge discoveries and "prescriptions" for how to get our beautiful brains and bodies to function even better.

Brendon Burchard: First, for sharing your own brush with death, which gave me the courage to share my own. Second, for motivating and even *pushing* me to share my Mind Loops programs with others – and to not allow my own perfectionism (a.k.a. fear) to stop me from releasing programs (and books like this one) when they have the ability to help so many people. Third, for being such a fantastic role model! You constantly demonstrate generosity, humility and cheerfulness – no matter how uber-successful and busy you are.

This book couldn't have been written without all the "De-Loopers" I've had the honor of working with: The "Detox Your Mind" and "Mind Loops" course participants, and especially the amazing clients in my private mentoring program. Thank you for your trust in me, for sharing your lives and stories with me, and for your courage to find ever-expanding ways to develop yourself, improve your own life and happiness – and make this world better as a result.

To all the baristas at my favorite Starbucks (you know the one) who juiced me up with coconut milk "Flat Whites" daily for months on end while I wrote this book! Your smiles and cheerfulness kept me going even when I felt exhausted.

My brilliant Mastermind partners – Wayne Lehrer and Michele Padgette – who have inspired, motivated, consoled, and cheered me on for three years (and counting). It's been an honor to show up weekly with you and watch each of us continue to transform for the better, share our newest, greatest discoveries about how to live and BE better in this world – and also be reminded of who we were when we started our group, and how far we've all come.

H.P., you know I couldn't have done this without you. Thank you from the bottom of my heart!

And finally to my wacky, creative, and loving family, Evelyn Daly, Joe Ireland, and Ben Ireland. I'm so thankful I was born into such a fascinating (and not for a *moment* boring!) family. Thank you for believing in me, loving me, and supporting my creativity from Day One. I love you all!

ABOUT THE AUTHOR

BARBARA IRELAND struggled with "Mind Loops" – repetitive, self-limiting thoughts – for years. During a near-death-experience in 2010, she was "taught" what Mind Loops were and how much they were holding her life and happiness hostage. She developed the "9 D's of De-Looping" system to *erase* and *replace* destructive, negative thoughts, and now helps others overcome self-doubt, self-criticism, fear, worry and other repetitive, self-defeating thoughts and emotions.

Ireland is founder of the Mind Loop Group in Seattle, WA. She is also a musician, singer and composer, award-winning filmmaker, and collage artist. She invites readers to email her at: barbara@themindloopgroup.com.

Made in the USA
Middletown, DE
16 January 2017